THE SOCIAL WORLD OF OLD WOMEN

Volume 78, Sage Library of Social Research

SAGE LIBRARY OF SOCIAL RESEARCH

THE SOCIAL WORLD OF OLD WOMEN

MANAGEMENT OF SELF-IDENTITY

SARAH H. MATTHEWS

Preface by JOHN LOFLAND

Volume 78
SAGE LIBRARY OF
SOCIAL RESEARCH

SAGE PUBLICATIONS   Beverly Hills / London

For information address:

SAGE PUBLICATIONS, INC.
275 South Beverly Drive
Beverly Hills, California 90212

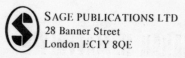

SAGE PUBLICATIONS LTD
28 Banner Street
London EC1Y 8QE

Printed in the United States of America

Library of Congress Cataloging in Publication Data

Matthews, Sarah H
    The social world of old women.

    (Sage library of social research; v. 78)
    Bibliography: p.
    1. Aged women--Social conditions. 2. Self-perception. 3. Identity (Psychology) I. Title.
HQ1061.M35   301.43'5   78-26723
ISBN 0-8039-1225-0
ISBN 0-8039-1226-9 pbk.

THIRD PRINTING, 1982

For my parents
Florence Swift Matthews
and
Ralph Bernard Matthews
Had I chosen them, I could not have done better.

CONTENTS

PREFACE

In this lucid and sensitive monograph, Dr. Matthews makes a signal contribution to the complex and evolving efforts of social scientists to lay bare the socially constructed character of precarious and stigmatized social and personal identities. A fundamental tenet of the reality-constructionist perspective on identity is that the labels and treatment that create social categories of humans create situations toward which people have to act as much as or more than they reveal biological, psychological, or other "kinds of people." Especially in the case of identities socially defined as shameful or defective, the conduct of their bearers needs importantly to be understood in terms of the disadvantaged social situations created by the labels and treatments themselves as against some in-born or other enduring aspects of persons.

The identity-constructionist perspective has been applied with enormous insight and social consequence to a wide variety of stigmatized identities in modern society. Applications to racial and sexual categories have been most notable over the past generation in America. Even a stigmatized identity that is common-sensically most "inward," that of mental illness, has come under decisive identity-constructionist scrutiny, most famously by Thomas Szasz in his *The Myth of Mental Illness.* The most generalized and far-reaching statement of the perspective is, perhaps, Erving Goffman's *Stigma,* a volume which comes as close to being the "bible" of identity-constructionist thought as anything now in print.

Well-versed in the identity-constructionist legacy, Dr. Matthews has, in this wide-ranging monograph, boldly addressed
yet another shameful subordination in what seems to be a
dismally long list—that of oldness. She does so with subtlety
and sophistication, noting that oldness differs in some ways
from other stigmatized identities, and making effective use of
macro-social and historical materials—aspects not ordinarily
treated in close studies of micro-interaction and the self.

A great many of the sad but classic themes of stigma
emerge among the old women she observed and interviewed:
a tendency to avoid seeing oneself as "one," an objective
deficit of social resources, efforts to mute the realization that
one is "one," and so forth.

The accumulation of so many studies of people who labor
under a category of socially shameful difference and who
manifest such a wide variety of remarkably similar strategic
alignments to their situation despite otherwise being enor-
mously different, itself lends considerable credence to the
reality-constructionist view of identity. Old women, the
retarded, the physically handicapped, the diverse sexual vari-
ants, racial minorities, and so on seem, indeed, interaction
kin under the social skin. In the case so powerfully portrayed
here, we are led directly to separate aging as a biological
phenomenon from oldness as a significantly arbitrary and
thoroughly social construct.

Adopting a comparative perspective on stigmatized identities and assuming a decades-long view of their histories, we
can quite easily see that such categories of persons vary
through time in the degree to which their occupants, as a
dominant motif of action, are willing quietly to labor under
the shame of their situation. The portrait of stratagems Dr.
Matthews etches in such loving detail also typifies quite well
the quiescent and minor-muttering stage seen historically
among other stigmatized groups—that early stage in which
the stigmatized acquiesce to the portrait of the shameful
defects imputed to them by dominant social groups.

The experiences of recent decades in America show, however, that acquiescence and minor mutterings are part of but one possibility. Another possibility, as is well known, puts forth several themes of assertiveness, pride, consciousness raising, solidarity, protest, and self-determination. If oldness is, indeed, as much or more a social construct than a biological state, we ought at least to envision the possibility of militant ideas and programs emerging with force and as a *dominant motif* among the old. The materials Dr. Matthews reports in her last chapter on conflicts endemic to senior citizen centers and to other community settings suggest the possibility that the early—social unrest—phases of such a new stage may already be underway. Ironically, the very officials sponsoring the stigma notion of oldness have already created an important part of the mobilization base for the emergence of militant oldness: the vast network of senior citizen centers and services that have so recently come on to the American social landscape. Such ironic government sponsorship and, therefore, organizing facilitation also underlie many of the identity revolts of the 1960s and the more recent ones among the physically and developmentally handicapped. Moreover, in the case of the old there is the potent and added ingredient of abundant leisure time.

In sum, in reading the experiences Dr. Matthews analyzes so faithfully and beautifully, one should be attuned to the imputed identity accidents of existence as much as to one or another notion of character or essence.

In this context it is important to discuss a second matter, one that rises directly from the first and is a consequence of it. Participants in a social world subjected to a social analysis *of* that world (as distinct from mere managerial analysis *in* that world) are frequently not happy with what social scientists say, especially social scientists of an identity-constructionist bent. And well they ought not to be.

All of us in our ordinary lives do (and likely must) develop self-serving beliefs—beliefs that while often true as far as they go omit certain critical aspects of life that would be disturbing to confront. And most of us most of the time have the civility to leave others alone in their more or less distorted notions. Now comes the social scientist whose task it is (among other tasks) to decipher how life goes on. To do that is, in fact, to have rather bad manners, to point out people's defects, as it were, by calling attention to their patterned avoidances and their conveniently self-serving rhetoric, as does Dr. Matthews with regard to, for example, old women's views of their oldness, family members' treatment of their old relatives, and official government ideologies of oldness.

The tension thus generated is further fueled by the fact that a first-rate social science analysis performs this impoliteness not to muckrake (an understandable attack against which one can defend) but, rather, as a phase in a most murky and arcane kind of process—the process of developing and elaborating systems of ideas and concepts, the project of constructing social theory. The raw and private unique aspects of the participants are sorted and grouped into abstract categories and conceived as instances of transcending social processes. The warm and shrouded provincial enclave formed by a sector of social life gets lifted onto the cold and open cosmopolitan terrain of generalized theory. In the present case, Dr. Matthews lifts "oldness" and its gerontological baggage out of its specialty pocket and places it in the vast and generic framework of stigma and identity. Such an act is easily (and properly) felt by participants—especially "professional" participants—to be arrogant and "unfeeling." The accumulated views and analytic devices participants feel to be *true* are, by implication, reduced to merely *a* view, a set of things to be bracketed and analyzed. Such a demotion can hardly be welcomed saved by the malcontents of a social world.

Despite such tensions, there can, of course, be liberation—for cognitive schemes likely differ in how hard they have to

labor in avoiding inconvenient matters. Some carry a heavy
load. In such cases, new analytic bracketings can be a release,
a way of beginning anew. Moreover, Dr. Matthews's brack-
eting is clearly concilliatory. Hers is definitely a social science
of aging rather than a social science *in* aging, but a social
science suffused with sympathy for all the participants, with
good will and with hope. It is my hope that readers involved
with oldness—which is all of us—also appreciate these latter
qualities despite the discomforts unavoidably experienced in
being the object of social science.

John Lofland
Davis, California

SERIES EDITOR'S PREFACE

Sarah Matthews' work, *The Social World of Old Women: Management of Self Identity*, links the foci of a variety of substantive fields in current social science. It deals with the social world of old people, but raises issues which affect all who are stigmatized and rendered powerless in our society.

Her subjects seem caught in a tangled web of cultural stereotypes, status contradictions, and, last but not least, policies designed to solve the problem of the aged. The women in this book attempt to fight back against those forces which tend to label them, indiscriminately, as useless or socially irrelevant. The strategies they adopt for their defense are a major focus of Dr. Matthews's research.

Despite its emphasis on the problematic aspects of the world of elderly women, this is not a "self-help" type of book. It does, however, conclude with a set of ideas that directly confront those groups and individuals who are trying to come to terms with the final stage in the human life cycle. It reminds us of the simple fact that this social category currently contains more than ten percent of the American population, and ultimately will enlist all of us who are destined to grow old.

Jetse Sprey
NCFR Monograph Editor

ACKNOWLEDGMENTS

In the end, writing this book has been a lonely endeavor, but it would not have been possible without the intellectual and emotional support of a great many people. To John Lofland I owe the greatest debt of gratitude for providing guidance and the framework without which I might still be floundering in a sea of ideas and data. For their comments on earlier drafts I thank Marcella Z. Davis, Bruce Hackett, Lyn H. Lofland, Julius A. Roth, Ellen Horgan Biddle, Harold B. Freshley, and Jetse Sprey. All were helpful in their reviews and the book owes much to their critical comments. I especially thank Juanita B. Wood and Kathleen M.G. Copp for the many hours of conversations we shared. Without their enthusiasm I am sure that the motivation to complete the book would have waned. I thank my fellow participants in the Midwest Council for Social Research in Aging who, under the tulelage of Warren A. Peterson, succeeded in making the research experience less isolating, more communal. Although the informants must go nameless, I thank them for sharing their lives with me and I hope that this book might contribute in some way to improving the lives of the old now and in the future.

This research was supported in part by a grant from the Administration on Aging, Department of Health, Education and Welfare. Researchers undertaking such projects are encouraged to express freely their professional judgment.

Therefore, points of view or opinions stated in this book do not necessarily represent the official position or policy of the Department of Health, Education and Welfare. Revisions were made while I held a postdoctoral fellowship in gerontology from the National Institute of Mental Health.

Chapter 1

INTRODUCTION

This book is a "close up" look at the social worlds of old women. It is intended to give the reader a better understanding of what being old is like by elucidating the social forces that impinge on those worlds and the ways actors mediate those forces. To this end it will, hopefully, prove useful to three overlapping audiences. First, those who are now experiencing old age and those who are concerned about their own old age will profit from seeing these social forces layed bare. People regard their own lives as unique, and rightly so. At the same time it is helpful to be aware of the broader picture, in that awareness often increases options for action. In the words of Berger (1963: 152), "Only he [or she] who understands the rules of the game, is in a position to cheat." By clarifying the rules of the "game," "being an old, widowed mother," it is hoped that the rules will no longer be able to wield power arbitrarily over unsuspecting social actors.

The increasing number of professionals who regard the aged as their clients is the second group who will profit from reading this close up look at the social worlds of old widows. After reading this book, they will, hopefully, have a better understanding of their clients and a keener insight into the most effective ways to offer assistance to them.

The third audience to whom this book is of interest is sociologists, social gerontologists, and other behavioral scientists who regard the aged as their research population. The research presented here challenges the taken-for-granted assumptions about old people upon which much research is currently based. Chronological age, along with gender, ethnicity, and social class, is considered to be a variable that explains behavior, one that must be "controlled" when groups are compared. It is widely recognized and accepted— although the nature-nurture debate, admittedly, is far from settled—that gender, ethnicity, and social class are not programmed in biology, but are socially constructed (Berger and Luckmann, 1967) and perpetuated through social interaction which maintains social institutions. Age, however, continues to be seen as composed largely of biological components. Recent research on childhood and adolescence has undermined the assumption of the "naturalness" of these age categories (Aries, 1962; Musgrove, 1965; Kett, 1977), but the assumption of the "naturalness" of old age being legitimately based in biology lives on, for the most part, unchallenged. Old age is seen as part of the "life cycle . . . defined in biology" (Atchley, 1976: 155).

The research presented here stands as a challenge to the notion of the "naturalness" of old age as a social category defined in biology. By putting aside taken-for-granted assumptions about old age, the social worlds of old widows in American society can be seen not as dictated by physical and mental decline, but as shaped by social and historical forces. The informants for this research are social actors defined as old by the society in which they live and forced to deal with the social meaning of their chronological age and with institutions based on those meanings. The research makes clear the overriding importance of the social rather than the biological meaning of their chronological age. Indeed, the informants' methods of coping with a less than desirable social situation are not peculiar to them, but are both familiar and ingenious and point to the similarities between social actors, rather than to differences that can be attributed to the informants' advanced years. Responses that are attributed to "senility" or "conservativeness" or any other of the myriad of explanations for "old" behavior can be more accurately viewed as methods of protecting self-image in threatening situations.

Overview

The analysis begins by setting the stage, first from a social-structural perspective and then from the "everyday-life" perspective (Douglas, 1974) in which the social structure is maintained and changed. The current societal definitions of old have arisen from a variety of historic and social trends, so that the position of the aged is now framed by economic and social forces that tend to limit options for participation in society. From a social-psychological perspective, oldness is an attribute that is discrediting, a stigma (Goffman, 1963), but a stigma with a few peculiarities. A discussion of oldness from these two perspectives will comprise Chapters 2 and 3.

After setting the stage, analysis will focus on methods of protecting the self in four problematic situations with which old, widowed mothers in American society must cope.

Human action . . . is directed to dealing with whatever is identified as problematic, as requiring that action be taken in one kind of situation or another. Situations are often situations *because* they present themselves as requiring some kind of preventive, remedial, reparative, corrective, or other circumstance-altering effort [Lofland, 1976: 40].

These efforts are referred to as strategies, "lines of action in situations" (Lofland, 1976: 42).

The focus of the analysis is on the informants' definitions of those situations, that is, on self (or ego) identity rather than social identity (Goffman, 1963). In so doing, it follows Davis's (1961: 132) conjecture in his research on deviance disavowal:

> it may be useful to consider whether, and to what extent, the deviator himself is not also engaged, albeit ineffectively, in somehow trying to sustain a normal definition of his person.

In the four situations presented here, the old widow risks being seen and seeing herself as a worthless, old woman, a state she prefers to avoid. Of course, in her preference she is not alone. Few people prefer feeling worthless to seeing themselves as valuable, a point that will be elaborated upon in each chapter. The four situations that require strategies to avoid negative definitions of self are:

(1) situations in which the old woman finds similarities between herself and the stereotypical old woman;
(2) settings in which the old woman has either aged or come to be already old;
(3) extended families in which old women are now old mothers and grandmothers;
(4) the situation of knowing that death is imminent.

Each of these situations and the strategies employed to cope with them is the subject of a chapter.

In addition, the generic features of each situation will be discussed. Old women are not atypical because of their age, but are similar to other members of society in their ability to develop strategies to cope with personally threatening situations. The situations are not the exclusive property of the aged but ones in which other members of society also find themselves. By attending to the generic features of each situation, readers will be better able to relate the situation of being old to other daily life situations in order to gain valuable insights into the nature of being in general and of being old in particular. The specific situations that the old widows confront are each an instance of the following more general situations:

(1) situations in which actor has a different definition of her or his identity than is held by others;

(2) situations in which taken-for-granted settings that support self-identity are removed;

(3) situations in which the actor has a high investment in a group in which s/he has few power resources;

(4) situations in which the actor attempts to take into account unknowable features of future situations.

The final chapter is an analysis of the interaction between the staff and the participants at a senior citizens center. By shifting analysis to ongoing interaction between those representing the societal view of old age and the old themselves who have very different views, an understanding of the way in which the social identity of the aged is constructed and perpetuated in everyday life will be gained.

Before proceeding it is necessary to convince the reader that the findings presented in the following chapters are grounded in a sound data base, and it is to this end that the remainder of this chapter is addressed.

Getting Close

When I began examining the social science literature on old people, I found that most of the research is either aimed at discovering the correlates of a "good adjustment" to old age or conducted principally to answer questions related to social policy. I came away from the literature feeling that I "knew about" old people in that I knew many objective facts, but that I did not "know" what being old is (Lofland, 1971). In

order to accomplish the latter, I chose to do qualitative
research to gain "intimate familiarity" (Lofland, 1976) with
the social worlds of old widows.

Qualitative methods to acquire "intimate familiarity" principally include two techniques: participant observation and
intensive interviewing. Both were used to gather data for this
research for reasons that will be discussed below, but, first,
the purpose and form of this style of data collection requires
elucidation.

> To be intimately familiar with a sector of social life is to have
> easy, detailed, dense acquaintanceship with it based on free-
> flowing and prolonged immersion. This immersion, first and ide-
> ally, may take the form of direct, bodily presence in the physical
> scenes of the social life under scrutiny, either in an indigenous
> role or in the role of someone known to be studying that world.
> This relation is known technically to a social scientist as "partici-
> pant-observation." . . . Though not ideal, a practical degree of
> intimate familiarity can often be attained by a second means—
> namely, long, diverse, open-ended, semistructured conversations
> with people who are participants in a situation or social world.
> Since some kinds of situations are not readily amenable to direct
> physical participation by analysts of them, selected participants
> must be induced to sit down for many hours, to discuss a wide
> range of concrete matters they confront and to talk about how
> they act toward them. Unlike more conventional "interviewing,"
> which is oriented importantly to attitudes, "intensive interview-
> ing" is oriented to collecting instances and episodes of action and
> instances and episodes of problems and how they are dealt with.
> A goal of intensive or "qualitative" interviewing is to construct
> records of action-in-process from a variety of people who have
> likely performed these actions time and time again. Key features
> of such "conversations" are their length and diversity. Unhurried,
> free-flowing talk encourages the emergence of a wide range on
> many levels of topics, prompting intimate familiarity [Lofland,
> 1976: 8-9].

Participant observation and intensive interviewing were
combined to "get close" to old widows, because being a

particular age, in this case "old," like being a particular
gender or ethnicity, colors every aspect of people's lives and
is, therefore, not confined to a setting.
Gathering qualitative data about "oldness," then, has several inherent obstacles. Although old women tend to congregate in specifiable places, these places are often informal and
require participants to be close friends and, a corollary, old.
In addition, the conversations that occur in more accessible
settings are infrequently related directly to oldness. They are,
instead, related to the ongoing activities of the setting. Further, a designation of themselves as "old" is refuted by many
old people, so that asking direct questions about their oldness
is either met by platitudes or incomprehension. These factors
combine to make participant observation time-consuming
and intensive interviewing—because it requires that old informants focus on an attribute that they would like to think of
as unimportant—a somewhat painful and confusing activity
for both the interviewer and the informant. As the following
review of data collection will make clear, the combination of
participant observation and intensive interviewing allows the
data to be more firmly grounded than would be true if only
one method for gathering data had been used.

Data Collection

The data under analysis here were gathered using four
methods: participant observations, "hired hand" intensive
interviews, intensive interviews, and archives. What each
method entailed will be briefly described.

PARTICIPANT OBSERVATION

My plan was to find some place to "hang out" with old
people to find out what they talked about, what they
thought about their worlds, and what they considered most
salient about being old. There are few places which are
nominally defined as places where old people congregate.
Senior citizens centers are notable exceptions, and I began

(December 1972) by talking with the supervisor of senior
citizens programs in a community of 30,000. He responded
to my request to be a volunteer by designating me assistant
to the housing authority representative, giving me legitimate
reason to be at the center one afternoon a week and, because
my face became familiar, to drop in at other times as well.
Fortuitously, a thirty-unit housing project for senior citizens
was scheduled to open in February, so there was a good deal
of interaction between the representative and the new
tenants and applicants, both at the Center and at the housing
project after it opened. This role allowed me to listen to old
people at the same time that I was becoming familiar with
the activities and politics of the Senior Center and the community. During this period of time it became clear to me
that, although the most straightforward research plan would
have been to study a setting, either the Senior Center or the
housing project, my interest in the general question of how
social actors do "old woman" remained.

In June 1973, there was an opening on the Senior Center
staff for the position of Activities Coordinator. I applied for
the part-time job, was hired, and worked there for over seven
months. I did not hide the fact that I was a graduate student
interested in gerontology, but no one was particularly interested. To the rare further questions, I explained that I was
tired of reading books on the subject and wanted to get some
first-hand knowledge. As activities coordinator I was responsible for arranging classes, one-day bus trips, and other center-
sponsored activities, and completing necessary details to
guarantee that all scheduled activities occurred smoothly.
The supervisor had final say over all aspects of my job, and
for the most part I merely carried out plans already on the
drawing board. My part-time job turned into a three-quarter
time job when the supervisor resigned and was not replaced
for four months. My responsibilities were greater: I was "the
boss," but the Center was a going concern at that point and I
was able to remain in the background. I continued to live in

the community after resigning from the job and dropped in at the Center from time to time.

When I first became involved with the setting I took systematic field notes on everything I could remember, but when I eliminated the possibility of an organizational study, I began to take notes only on old women's conversations with each other, with staff members, and with me, paying special attention to their references to oldness, relationships with others, daily rounds, and dying and death. I made notes to myself at work, usually verbatim, which I typed in triplicate with situational details before I returned the next day.

Data collected through participant observation in the community setting gave me many insights into the everyday worlds of old women that are not apparent in interview situations. Observing and interacting with the same women for over a year provided data on which parts of their social worlds were most important and which parts most problematic. In addition, I was not a stranger to them, but eventually a trusted person who could share in their backstage, at least to some degree.[1] I was also able to test the accuracy of my perceptions of their views of the world. Often the fallacies of my taken-for-granted assumptions were abruptly made clear to me by comments that changed the meanings I had assigned to behavior and words. In short, although participant observation was time consuming and often frustrating, it was an invaluable portion of the research.

"HIRED HAND" INTENSIVE INTERVIEWS[2]

In February 1973, I was contacted by a person in a metropolitan area with whom I had spoken a few months previously. He was concluding a two-year research project using questionnaires on a large sample of old people who had applied, sometimes successfully, for public housing. He was coming to the end of his fiscal year and had money left that was earmarked for his research staff. He invited me to use his interview staff to carry out a project of my own and so I

quite unexpectedly was presented with five trained interviewers to do research for me. I chose to train them to do
intensive interviewing with white, widowed mothers over 70
years of age wo lived alone. We had half a dozen training
sessions, following Lofland's (1971) guide to qualitative analysis, in which I explained the purpose and mechanics of
intensive interviewing and the kind of data in which I was
interested. The discussion included many questions that
appear in the interview guide that I used (Appendix II), but
during their interviews they used only the guide that appears
in Appendix I. Their basic instructions were to engage in a
conversation based on the interview guide and to continue
the conversation as long as possible. The interviews were
tape-recorded and vary in length from one hour to four
hours, with the majority being one and one-half hours. The
informants were chosen from the list of applicants already
interviewed and were each paid five dollars. The data used in
this paper include thirty-one of these interviews.

Although I had misgivings about the quality, the data
collected in this fashion proved to be very valuable. Essentially what I have on tape are recorded conversations between
old widows and younger persons (aged 30-45). The tapes
show that I was successful in convincing each interviewer that
the only way to fail to satisfy me was to conduct a short
interview and to give too many of her own opinions, that is,
to "lead" the informant in some way. Thus, I was able to
collect in a short period of time a great deal of conversational
data. The main disadvantage is that the interviewers did not
always probe as carefully as I would have liked, and that the
content of each interview is in no way dependent on the
previous interviews, as is ideal in intensive interviewing
(Glaser and Strauss, 1967). My transcriptions and analysis of
the recorded interviews, however, as I listened to each one,
were dependent on previously collected data and interviews.

PERSONAL INTERVIEWS

During the course of gathering data, I conducted seven intensive interviews with widowed mothers aged 68+ which lasted at least an entire morning or afternoon. Five of the informants I met through the Senior Center, although only one was active in Center activities. The other two informants had no connection with the Center. The interview guide which I used is shown in Appendix II. Many of the questions were confusing to the informants, even though they were based in previous data I had collected. After several attempts to use it, I reverted to the simpler one (Appendix I). The fact that the questions were awkward had little effect on the informants' willingness to talk, however, and they usually answered all my questions in their own time. All the formal questions are about oldness, a state that the old woman prefers not to acknowledge to herself. The strong element of denial that her own behavior is related in any way to her age, makes straightforward questions about her age very disrupting to the conversational flow. The tactic used in the "hired hand" interview guide, which is essentially to encourage the informant to talk—for the most part about daily activities and relations with others—appeared to be the better one.

I typed the interviews in triplicate, as I did the field notes, verbatim when they related to oldness, relations with others, death and dying, and daily rounds. Material that seemed unrelated, I merely summarized.

ARCHIVES

A fourth source of data was the written word. Novels, feature newspaper articles, advice columns, autobiographies, were all viewed as legitimate data concerning taken-for-granted assumptions about the social meaning of oldness, and were gleaned for ideas and data about oldness.

Data Analysis

I started almost immediately to do tentative analysis of my data following the "grounded theory" approach outlined by Glaser and Strauss (1967) and the techniques set forth by Lofland (1971, 1976) in his guides to qualitative analysis. At that time I began cutting up data and filing together bits that seemed to be alike. My data were organized according to categories similar to the interview guide so that I had, for example, old widows' comments on relationships with sons and daughters, grandchildren, friends, younger persons, and strangers. These relationships are all parts of the social worlds of the informants. It was not until I began to see the importance of strategies for preserving self-identity in various situations emerge that I could see a framework grow out of the data.

My first framework included "talk" and "role ambiguity" as key concepts. When I tried to flesh it out, I could see where and why it was unsuitable. One of my original interests was in definitions of old. I wanted to know what old people's working definitions were. A great deal of my early efforts at analysis were directed toward finding a framework in which I could place statements about oldness. I found that "ambiguity" in the definition of old is never resolved, in part, because it never needs to be. Oldness is not a pivotal self-identity (Lofland, 1969:121ff.) for most old people and, therefore, does not require a consistent definition. The lack of a definition proved more interesting. Definitions of oldness are situational. In addition, there is no commitment to a single, consistent definition because old people prefer to think that they are not old. Flexibility in the definition is an advantage. If old persons are free to change the definition at will, they will be able to avoid more easily applying the label to themselves.

The two theories that are used to clarify the meaning of oldness to the social actors, exchange theory and labeling theory, under whose heading the concept of stigma falls, were chosen because they seemed to me to fit the data, to lay bare the forces that were operating. I am sure that I share with other social scientists the fear that I have imposed theory on data, but much data and soul searching has helped to allay that fear for me. I hope that I have not done my informants an injustice.

The Question of Generalizability

The informants for this research do not constitute a random sample. The question may be raised, then, to whom are the findings generalizable? A great many variables were controlled by choosing as informants white widows over 70 years of age who live alone and are mothers. Social class was not controlled. None of my informants is a member of a "classical extended family" (Litwak, 1960; Townsend, 1957).

My original assumption was that old age is a more powerful characteristic for my particular research interests than social class. The losses that accompany old age, for the most part, are not mitigated by high social class, especially for widows. Had I been interested, for example, in specific leisure pursuits, social class would have been an important variable, but I was interested in social-psychological aspects of being old. I am satisfied that my assumption was correct. Other distinctions, for example, newcomer and resident, were much more important.

Gathering data at a senior citizens' center and from a pool of public housing applicants may appear to be biased in the direction of lower-middle and lower-class women, but an examination of the social class background of the informants refutes this. Widows who gather at senior citizens' centers across the land are, to point to the obvious, drawn from the communities in which the centers are located. The community in which I worked and lived was predominantly middle and upper-middle class and the participants at the Center reflected the community. In addition, there was enough diversity in the activities at the Center so that a wide variety of women was attracted.

Contrary to expectations, the informants who were housing project applicants are also not predominantly lower class. Incomes for old widows are not a reflection of incomes in middle-age. As a group, old widows are the poorest of all old people. Since the widows interviewed by hired hand interviewers had been interviewed earlier, social class data were available for them. They represent a wide range of social classes in middle years, although both the very poor and the very rich are missing. The use of the t-test to compare the social class of the 14 informants who qualified for public housing with the 17 who did not revealed no difference between the two groups. The obvious difference between the two groups of women was the age at which they were widowed. Twelve of the 14 who qualified for public housing were widowed before they were 50,[3] and 14 of the 17 who did not were widowed after they were 60. This reflects not social class, but the difference between wages for males and females and therefore, differences in social security benefits and eligibility for pensions. The question of representativeness of the informants, however, is largely irrelevant for the analysis that follows is of "how," not "why," social actors deal strategically with problematic situations.

A Word of Caution

One final note of caution is in order before analysis begins: qualitative strategy analysis (Lofland, 1976) focuses on strategies social actors use to deal with problematic situations. There is a danger that actors will be represented as being more consciously manipulative and having more problems than is actually the case from their subjective viewpoints. The strategies presented in the following pages are not always consciously planned, but regardless of conscious awareness, they affect social interaction in such a way that the outcome is protection of the old widows' self-identities. In addition, the problematic situations presented are not overwhelming for all the informants: the strategies they employ to protect self-identities are, for the most part, successful. My conjecture is that protection of self-identity is precarious for all social actors and that a detailed analysis of anyone's strategies for protection of self makes obvious the precariousness of our own images of ourselves. "Getting close" to powerful persons, rather than "deviants" and "underdogs," is difficult, and until such a time as there are role-scale studies of protection of self-image among more powerful social actors this conjecture must remain an untested hypothesis.

NOTES

1. A person in her or his twenties who prefers to spend time with old people who are nonrelatives instead of age peers is somewhat "suspect." On a three-day outing with my "old women" friends, I was encouraged by them to spend time with a group of younger women in attendance who were strangers to me rather than with the old women with whom I had come. Similarity in age was frankly regarded as a stronger tie than friendship. During the course of data-gathering, the age-segregated nature of American society was made very clear to me: I had to go out of my way to encounter old women in my daily rounds.

2. "Hired hand" is borrowed from Roth (1966: 195) who employs the term to describe

a person who feels that he has no stake in the research that he is working on, that he is simply expected to carry out assigned tasks and turn in results which will "pass inspection." Of course, a hired assistant may not start out with the hired hand mentality, but may develop it if he finds that his talents for creativity are not called upon and that his suggestions and efforts at active participation are ignored.

Whether or not the interviewers perceived themselves as merely hired hands was not formally ascertained. From the standpoint of time, the project was short enough so that the hired hand mentality was, hopefully, avoided.

3. Measuring the social class of women who are not attached economically to a male has been largely ignored in research on social stratification until recently (McClendon, 1976).

Chapter 2

THE SOCIETAL CONTEXT OF OLD AGE

The social-psychological aspects of being old cannot be focused upon accurately before the larger social context within which being old occurs is considered. The old adage, "You are as young as you feel," may appear to the individual to be true only because the forces of the larger social structure are hidden, making the similarities between situations in which people find themselves less obvious. These unseen forces mark the parameters of any socially defined characteristic.

In all likelihood, old has come to be associated directly with chronological age only in the last fifty years. In societies in which there is no specified retirement age and childbearing is likely to continue into the early forties, old is probably associated with health and physical ability rather than age per se. In nineteenth-century America, persons were considered old when they were no longer physically able to participate in their social worlds (Hareven, 1977). Even though the legal

definition of old is now based on chronological age, the
assumption that ill health and physical infirmity invariably
accompany old age is still made (Shanas, 1962). "Even those
who survive into old age without physical handicaps are
stereotyped as incapable."

> Old people are classed . . . with children and the handicapped, on
> the assumption that people in these categories must be regarded
> as dependents and that society as a whole has a responsibility to
> assure that all who are dependent are not deprived of some
> measure of assistance [Lakoff, 1976: 645].

The number of accumulated years required to be legally old,
that is, to collect social security, has decreased from sixty-
five to sixty-two in the past two decades and has already
dropped into the fifties for some retirement programs,
making the assumed correlation between poor health and old
age even more questionable.

The relationship between years accumulated and chronic
disability is undeniable. Neugarten (1966: 177) cites statistics
which indicate that more than three-fourths of persons over
65 years of age have some chronic health condition. To bring
the figure into comparative perspective the reader is re-
minded that three-fifths of persons aged 45 to 64 years of age
have at least one chronic health condition. Physical limitations do not descend upon persons suddenly, but gradually,
throughout the aging process. As will be discussed in detail
below, most old people, although they may suffer from a
chronic health condition or two (or three or more), are not
physically incapacitated. "Only about 4 percent of old people reside in institutions of any kind, and about 82 percent of
the noninstitutionalized get along with no difficulty whatso-
ever" (Brody, 1971: 53).

Legally old, then, is closely associated with chronological
age, which is an indication of physical condition, but by no
means an infallible one. However, the correlation between
the two is taken to be perfect, and having lived sixty years or

more is now synonymous with physical and, therefore, economic dependence on other members of society. This may
not be true for each individual over sixty, but is "virtually" if
not "actually" true (Goffman, 1963: 2). The effect of social
legislation adopted in the 1930s during the Depression and
expanded into the 1970s has been to associate increased
chronological age with dependency (Friedmann, 1960). Old
age itself is defined as physically disabling, as evidenced by
the fact that the old, blind, and disabled are now considered
a homogeneous group in social legislation.

By attending to physical dependency rather than financial
dependency, the biological aspects of aging are emphasized
and the social meaning that has been assigned to chronological age is taken to be inherent in the numerical age itself. In
this chapter the historic, demographic, and social factors
which have shaped the current social definition of old age
will be explored. Briefly the argument is that industrialization and demographic changes made the labor contributions
of the old unnecessary. The assumption that old age is a time
of dependency due to inevitable biological decline was used
to legitimate social legislation. Once in place this legislation
promoted the social definition. In 1965, with the passage of
the Older Americans Act, this definition of old age was made
explicit. An assessment of the validity of the stereotype of
old persons, the three major components of the stereotype
being poverty, isolation, and ill health, will comprise the
remainder of the chapter.

The Social Construction of Oldness

The present social meaning of old has developed for a
variety of reasons that have little to do with biology. In
1900, only 4% of the population of the United States had
reached the age of 65. By 1930, over 5% of the population
was in this age group. Approximately 10% of the population
was over 65 in the 1970 census (Brotman, 1971: 2). Those

meeting the current chronological age requirement for old, then, have increased significantly, both proportionately and numerically, in this century.

At the same time, the economy has changed from one based on "low energy technology" to one based on "high energy technology" (Cottrell, 1960), making the need for the contributions of all able-bodied workers unnecessary. Compulsory education was instituted for the economically superfluous on one end of the age spectrum (Musgrove, 1965), superannuation for those on the other. As the individual's survival came to be based on trading time and skills for money (or depending financially on someone who was), being deemed ineligible for the labor market was to be deprived of the chance to share in the growing economic prosperity. Friedmann has pointed out that, in all likelihood, the economic position of the aged did not shift markedly with the advent of industrialization, but that their position in relation to the rest of society changed.

> The industrial promise of the early part of the century saw the concept of subsistence wage of classical economics replaced by the notion of the "fair" wage . . . which enabled the individual to share in the fruits of an expanding economy [Friedmann, 1960: 136].

At the same time, those defined as "old," the lower age limit of which fluctuated markedly during times of economic depression when jobs were scarce, were not allowed to participate—or could not participate—in the labor market and thus had no way of enjoying the expanded economy.

By the turn of the century employers had been established long enough to have employees who had worked for them many years and mutual feelings of responsibility had accrued. Brown (1950) parallels Musgrave (1965) in pointing out that superannuation, which first appeared around the turn of the century in the form of informal pensions and grants, the continuance of which was often arbitrary, were a way of legitimizing self-interest for the corporations. In addition, superannuation served younger members of the labor force by limiting the number of persons available for hire, thereby increasing their chances for a better paying, secure job, at least until they, too, joined the ranks of the aged. Thus, a high-energy technology and economic self-interest, although tempered slightly by "the force of expectancies in the employment relationship" (Brown, 1950: 66), combined to spell poverty for most old people.

The increasing proportion of the aged as well as their concentrated presence in urban areas which accompanied industrialization made their poverty more visible, but poverty was considered under the law and probably by most people to be a moral failing rather than a result of social arrangements. Until the Depression, the old ideology, first instituted in the Elizabethan Poor Laws, which served as one of the bases for state codes in the United States, was accepted. The Poor Laws combined two principles: first, the principle that poverty is an individual failing and, second, the principle of public responsibility for the support of the poor, albeit at a low economic level (tenBroek, 1964; Komisar, 1974). If old people who could no longer work were poverty stricken, it was due to lack of foresight: saving for old age had obviously been in order and those requiring financial assistance certainly deserved no more than a subsistence income, if that.

In the early years of the twentieth century, organized groups began to question this belief. A number of organizations, whose members, if not their leaders, were primarily old people, formed to demand pensions, the argument being that "the aged person had benefited society by working hard, paying taxes, and rearing children and that [society] should pay its debt to him with an old age pension" (Putnam, 1970: 9). However, in accepting aid from the state, people undermined their respectability.

In the ideological matrix of laissez-faire one might live on the bounty of the state, but one forfeited one's respectability in the process. If one sought to raise one's income by requesting state aid, one lowered one's status by accepting it [Putnam, 1970: 8-9].

Social legislation introduced in the wake of the Depression institutionalized the notion that poverty in old age, as in other groups, is as much a result of economic arrangements as it is an individual failing. At that time a network of public social services was put into operation, designed specifically to maintain the indigent aged, which now included all the aged, for they were, by definition, "too old to work."

Dependency and old age, then, became instrinsically and officially linked during the Depression. Those on the other end of the age spectrum were already officially dependent in that attending school precluded working, but they were the financial responsibility, at least ideally, of their parents. Those deemed too old to work were not so easily assigned to members of the labor force, especially during the Depression, when income for wage earners was far from secure.

In formulating the Social Security Act in the 1930s, a major concern was with the elimination of a segment of the population from the work force at a time when jobs were scarce (Brown, 1950). An unforseen consequence of this expeditious action was to institutionalize a social definition of old age as dependency.

The identification of the dependent aged and the developing of a network of services for them which occurred during the 1940's had the effect of identifying old age itself rather than dependency as the problem of the aged. *It further posited dependency, disability, and isolation as the normal expectation for the old in our society* [Friedmann, 1960: 139].

Advanced years are now seen as causing isolation, dependency, and disability, which is, of course, true, but in great part because of the manner in which old age is socially defined. The social definition "too old to work," rather than "old," led to isolation and dependency. Old age, however, is seen as the causal or independent variable and the intervening variables are ignored.[1]

This process of expediency continued into the 1960s with the passage of Medicare. In the 1950s advocates of national health insurance for the entire population changed their tactics to focus only on the aged (Corning, 1969). They reasoned that Congress and the public would be sympathetic to the plight of the aged and that once Medicare had been put into effect for the aged, national health insurance could more easily be extended to other groups. This plan, of course, had a better chance of success if emphasis were placed on the many medical and financial problems faced by the old.

The aged have undoubtedly benefited from Medicare and the Social Security Act, both of which have directly affected their standard of living. However, in serving as the means that justified others' ends, they have also suffered. The advocates of legislation have promoted an image of the aged as dependent members of society, dependent because they are no longer capable, primarily because of physical and mental incapacity, of participating in society as full-fledged adults. Their incapacities are assumed to be rooted, not in social arrangements but in a irreversible biological decline that begins sometime in middle-age.

The passage of both Social Security and Medicare was officially sold and legitimated on the premise that older persons are likely to have limited incomes. Both are specifically designed to deal with financial problems. The social definition of the old that they perpetuate is implicit. With the passage of the Older Americans Act in 1965 and its many titles (Administration on Aging, 1976), the social definition became explicit. Old age itself, not merely limited income, was officially legislated problematic.

The argument that unmet needs were distributed widely throughout the older population—*that they were not exclusive to older persons with low income*—had figured prominently in the deliberations of Congress leading to the passage of the Older Americans Act of 1965. Also, it was argued that the elderly would receive the attention they deserved only if their unmet needs were separated from the problems of other groups and action to deal with them was taken independently. In theory, the enactment of the Older Americans Act signified an alternative approach to the provision of social services to the elderly; the act was based on the approach of treating *all* the elderly as potential recipients of services [Gold, 1974: 65, emphasis added].

This new approach to problem-solving, as outlined in the Older Americans Act, then, is "aged-based" rather than "income-based" and old age itself is explicitly defined as a problem.

In summary, the argument presented here is that "old" has come to be increasingly associated with chronological age in this century. At the same time, "old" has maintained its traditional meaning of physical disability and biological decline. This definition was originally used to legitimate denying the old access to the labor market, thus making them financially dependent on younger members of society, but on the basis of age alone rather than physical disability. This process was greatly accelerated by the Depression and made obvious by the increasing number and proportion of the aged in the population. In 1965 the assumption was made explicit in the Older Americans Act in which old age itself, not physical incapacity or financial hardship, is officially legislated problematic. We will return to this theme in the final chapter where the argument will be made that a new stage in the life cycle, postadulthood, is in the process of being socially constructed.

Assessing the Stereotype

It has been suggested above that those people in American society who are old are unemployed and poor. To check the validity of these assertions, a presentation of the demographic variables that describe this age group is in order. As will become apparent in the discussion that follows, the differences in the statistical pictures of males and females in this age group are great enough that if the variable "sex" is not controlled, the picture is very misleading.

Aged persons in American society are often depicted as having barely enough money on which to survive, being socially isolated and forgotten by their families, being decrepit and in poor health, and struggling to fill meaningless days. Two headlines from front page feature articles in *The Wall Street Journal* are indicative: "Out to Pasture: To Be Old and Poor is to be Alone, Afraid, Ill-Fed, and Unknown," (Isenberg, 1972) and "Out to Pasture: The Old but Affluent Withdraw to Sun City to Fill Empty Days" (Lancaster, 1972). The general or statistical truth of these assumed characteristics, with the exception of the last, which is a more subjective imputed attribute, can be discovered by reviewing the results of previous studies of the aged population.

Are the Aged Poor?

As with many questions, the answer to this one is "yes and no." Researchers who focus on the older population are quick to admonish those who treat the aged as a homogeneous group. In a review of the literature on "Correlates of Satisfaction among the Aged," Adams (1971: 64) writes:

> Very few generalizations have been forthcoming which applied equally to males and females. If they had been combined, and treated as "old people," many of the "findings" would have been less obvious, if apparent at all. The sex differential represents but one major division of the "elderly" into more homogeneous groups for investigation. . . . It is the author's belief that an adequate theory of the aged and of aging will be developed only when major attention is given to such sub-group variation.

Still, the probability of someone's falling below the poverty level if s/he is 65 or over is much higher than for someone younger.

In 1970, when the official poverty level was $2,328 for couples, $1,852 for an individual living alone, approximately 25% of persons aged 65 and over had incomes below the poverty line. This percentage hides the wide range of difference between families and single persons. Fifteen percent of families headed by a person 65 or over and 47% of those living alone or with nonrelatives fell below the poverty line (Brotman, 1971: 8). Although not all old persons are officially poor, many who are not must live with the knowledge that any unexpected event, such as an increase in rent or food costs, or medical costs arising from extended illness, will undermine a comfortable but precarious financial position (Cooley and Cooley, 1965; Shanas, 1962). The last financial threat has been eliminated, at least in part, by the advent of Medicare and Medicaid, but the precarious balance of many older persons' budgets is still a source of insecurity. Rejoining or staying in the labor force is not a realistic option. This is especially true for women. Twenty-five percent of men aged 65 and over are still in the labor force, while only 10% of women in the same age group are employed (Siegel, 1972: 73).

Women living alone, i.e., approximately one-third of all women aged 65 and over, have the lowest median income of the aged population ($1,888 in 1970) [Siegel, 1972: 78]. Marriage as a possibility for "upward mobility" through combined incomes is not an option for most women in this age category for two reasons. Approximately 70% of men aged 65 and over are married, while two-thirds of women in the comparable age group are widowed, divorced, or single. For every 100 men who are 65 and over, there are 138 women, ranging from approximately 129 for the 65-74 age group to 156 for the 75+ age group (Brotman, 1971). Since traditionally women have married men who are slightly older than they, chances for remarriage are slim indeed. The reverse of this principle, that is, that men tend to marry women younger than themselves, accounts in part for the fact that men are less likely to be widowed, but in itself further reduces the chances of remarriage for women as they grow older.[2]

The financial picture for many of the old improved when the Supplemental Security Income Program (SSI) was established in 1974. This legislation changed Old Age Assistance, formerly each state's welfare program for the old, to a federally administered program thereby establishing a minimum income level for all the elderly irrespective of the states in which they resided. In 1975 these levels were $1,892 for individuals, $2,839 for couples who qualified by meeting a means test. States whose minimum payment was higher than the federal limit continue to pay the difference. In addition, both social security and SSI benefit levels are now tied to the economy so that there is an automatic cost-of-living increase. For most of the elderly, then, income is no longer "fixed," although states may reduce their contributions as benefit levels set on the national level are raised. Unfortunately, SSI has not been instituted long enough to gage its effects. Orshansky (in Schulz, 1976[b]: 568) notes:

> the SSI payment schedule with its differential for living alone may be large enough to coax out some new independent aged one- or two-person households, particularly those just approaching age 65 who are still pondering over living arrangements for their retirement years. We may, thus by providing better support for our older citizens, achieve the paradox of moving some of our now hidden aged poor—about 1.3 million persons, almost all women by latest counts—and raising the count of the needy.

Schulz (1976a), in assessing the economic position of the aged, is optimistic about their future financial situation. However, he sees the continuation of poverty among elderly women as a problem that is not currently being addressed.

Orshansky writes that "in our society, at every age and every stage, women are more vulnerable to poverty than men" (in Schulz, 1976[b] : 568). At this time, the social security system is under attack for a variety of reasons, but one is that it does not adequately reflect the position of women in society (Allan, 1975). The formula for establishing benefit levels assumes that women are not likely to be in the labor force. Because women are "dependents" of husbands and "survivors" when their husbands die, the benefits they receive are computed irrespective of their own contributions. Women who have worked and paid into social security may in some cases actually receive smaller benefits than women who have not worked but whose husbands' earnings were greater than the employed women's husbands'. A further complication is that "lower earnings and intermittant work histories are not uncommon among women. These two factors result in lower social security pensions (or in not qualifying for benefits at all)" (Schulz, 1976a: 160). Social security benefits are now reduced by one-third when women's husbands die. In addition, private pensions benefits are often reduced or discontinued when "the worker" dies, drastically reducing widows' incomes. Women, then, for a variety of reasons, are more likely to have lower incomes than men in old age. In sum, to have accumulated 65 years or more, then, is not synonymous with poverty, and there is evidence that the situation has greatly improved (Schulz, 1976a), but the probability of the two coinciding is high, especially for women. As Tissue (1972) has pointed out, low income itself may be a much more salient variable than advanced age per se in understanding the behavior of aged persons.

Are the Aged Isolated?

The correlates of growing old all spell out increasing degrees of social isolation. Old age is marked by the loss of children to homes of their own; retirement from jobs that involved the employed in relationships on and, sometimes, off the job; the loss of old friends to either death or distance, the latter of which makes meetings except by telephone difficult; and the loss of spouses to death. The old are excluded both purposely and by fate from roles and there is no concomitant inclusion in other roles to take their places (Rosow, 1974). The effect of loss of available roles, especially on women, will be discussed in more detail.

The responsibility of rearing children is over for most parents at earlier ages than in the past. Persons aged 65 and over in the mid-1970s became parents in the 1920s and 1930s, a period in American history that was marked by a sharp drop in the number of births (Siegel, 1972: 18). Fewer children and younger parents combined to introduce a new phase in the family life cycle, "post-parental life" (Deutscher, 1962). This stage is marked by the absence of children in the home and a reduction in the content of the roles of mother and father. This is seen as much greater loss to women, whose identity is viewed as more dependent on parenting (Donahue et al., 1960: 397-399), than to men, whose identity is seen as much more dependent on economic productivity. Indeed, a clear dichotomy emerges in the gerontological literature: the children's growing up and leaving the home is viewed as a woman's problem, while retirement is viewed as primarily problematic to men (Beeson, 1975). When it is not, the problem for women is having a retired man around the house. However, in the last twenty-five years, the rate of labor force participation for women has increased considerably. In 1955, 1960, 1965, and 1970, the years in which those considered old in 1975 would have worked, 32.5%, 38.3%, 41.4%, and 43.0% of women aged 55 to 64 were employed (Siegel, 1972: 76). While these rates were much lower than for men of comparable ages, the fact that more than two of every five women aged 55-64 were employed in 1970 indicates that retirement may no longer be an exclusively male problem.

The presence of a confidant, whether friend, offspring, relative, or spouse, has been shown to be an important requirement for "good mental health" and "high morale" for the aged: "the presence of an intimate relationship apparently does serve as a buffer against such decrements as loss of role or reduction of social interaction" (Lowenthal and Haven, 1968: 396-397). Unfortunately, confidants are not easily found. Whether this is specific to the aged alone or more generally true for all members of society is not clear (Arth, 1962), but there are certain hurdles that are peculiar to the aged. Death often claims the old person's confidants. As noted above, women are likely to be widows, and, thus, spouses are eliminated for many women as possible confidants. Blau (1961) has noted that widows are often socially isolated until their married friends become widowed also, so that loss of a husband may be compounded simultaneously by exclusion from friendship groups. Lopata's (1970) study of widows' adaptations to their husbands' deaths indicates that isolation is not a preferred adaptation but the only one available to a woman whose primary contact with others was through her husband. Rosow (1967) has pointed to the difficulty of establishing friendship ties between members of different age categories. Similarity in age, like similarity in gender, marital status, and social class, is a status attribute that promotes friendship formation. "Age dense" housing, that is, housing in which at least 50% of the occupants are old, affects opportunities for friendship among the aged. The opportunities are not uniform, however, because they are mediated by the personal life styles of the residents.

The question of whether or not the aged are forgotten by their families has been dealt with extensively in the last 25 years. The assumption that the aged were integrated members of extended families at the turn of the century and have lost much ground since then because of industrialization or modernization (Cowgill and Holmes, 1972), is often made.

In 1900 in an era still agricultural, the aged were generally persons of considerable power in the family because they controlled property and occupations, and they were greatly respected for their knowledge and ability. Since then, with the growth of our industrial society, property and jobs have moved away from family control. Increased physical mobility separates the aged more often from their children and other kin. The relationship of aged husband and wife has been strengthened by its prolongation and its equilitarian nature; but the older people now depend less on kin and more on government, industry, and philanthropy. The loss by the aged of economic power, authority, and deference within the family is probably the most important change in their family situation during the past half century [Nimkoff, 1962: 414].

By Nimkoff's own admission, however, his ideas are speculative.

An equally strong case can be made for the other side (Schorr, 1960). The opportunity for geographic mobility of the young was great in the nineteenth century, and once members of kinship groups were separated geographically, communication was much more difficult than it is today. Focusing on a single issue, Moore (1950: 36) writes of "the errors of romanticizing the extended family of the past."

> Comparisons of the ease of housing the aged in rural communities as contrasted with the cramped space in urban apartments are likely to involve unrecognized comparisons through time and across social strata. Not all rural families lived in large, rambling dwellings where aged parents may be given a room and a corner in a spacious living room. The spacious dwelling unit is a rarity in rural as in urban communities: Crowding is common in both.

Historical data to settle this empirical question are not readily available and the debate cannot be resolved; although as the topic of old age becomes more popular, historians are beginning to look at previously untapped materials (Fischer, 1977; Hareven, 1977). This debate is similar to the larger debate between those who feel that the position of the aged in agrarian societies is far better than in industrial societies, and those who argue that industrialization is not in itself a causal variable (Fischer and Stone, 1977). Human societies are not so cooperative as to arrange themselves along a neat continuum that accords the aged highest status in small agrarian societies and lowest status in postindustrial societies (McTavish, 1971; Cowgill, 1974).

In the past two decades, the nature of the extended family in American society has been documented. In 1942 Parsons advanced the theory that anything other than the nuclear family is dysfunctional in industrial societies. A growing lack of extended family relations was generally accepted as accurate. Although absence of extended family relations may have been true at some point in time, it seems more likely that excluding the aged by definition from studies of the family, precluded designing studies that would reveal the empirical nature of the kinship network. Beard (1949), in a review of twenty textbooks on marriage and the family, found only two with chapters on the aged. Eight made no mention of the aged in the table of contents or index and the remainder mentioned the aged only briefly. Care of the aged was seldom considered to be one of the functions of the family and the aged were most frequently spoken of as problems. When empirical research on the kinship network was begun in the late 1950s, an "academic culture lag" (Sussman and Burchinal, 1962) was revealed when the findings were compared with the then-current family theory. Research showed the existence of the "modified extended family," which consists of "a series of nuclear families bound together on an equalitarian basis, with a strong emphasis on the extended family bonds as an end value" (Litwak, 1960: 10).

Further research has shown that in most cases the old parent is not isolated from and ignored by his or her children. Blenkner (1965) maintains that the social myth of alienation of the old is perpetuated by professional workers who see only the aged who have no families or who have been alienated from them, perhaps one-fifth of the total population of people over sixty-five, and that this is a poor sample from which to make generalizations about all old people. Old parents living with offspring is less common than in the past. Over 80% of married couples, one of whom is aged 65 or over, live alone, while 50% of nonmarried persons aged 65 and over live alone, and, of importance here, 50% of widows live alone. In most cases, living alone appears to be by choice. One of the strongest correlates of the old parent or parents living with offspring is lack of funds to support two households (Bixby et al., 1975: 126-136; Schorr, 1960). Rising levels of Social Security benefits and other pension programs, the increase in the number of persons covered and for longer periods of time, and the rise in incomes generally, combine to make the option of maintaining a separate household a realistic possibility.[3] Most old people prefer to live near, but not with, their offspring (Shanas, 1962; Lopata, 1970), and this preferred state is quite common. In Shanas's (1962: 18) study "only about 15% of all older people with children—one in seven—said that their nearest child was as far from them as a day's travel or more." Other studies have confirmed this finding (Young and Geertz, 1961; Riley and Foner, 1968). Most old people, then, live in close geographical proximity to at least one of their children.

Again, the question addressed here—are the aged isolated—must be answered in terms of probabilities. Current social arrangements and deaths of role partners combine to reduce the number of roles available to the aged. This is more often true for women, for whom retirement, widowhood, and living alone are much more likely, than for men. The "modified extended family" may serve as a buffer to these other assaults, but how much of one is not clear from survey data alone and will be the subject of Chapter 6.

Are the Aged Decrepit and in Poor Health?

In the section above which dealt with the social construction of oldness, the assumed strong correlation between old age and ill health was discussed. The time has come to consider the validity of that assumption. As is true of most stereotypes, the one that depicts old people as ill and decrepit holds some truth, but by no means all, or even a majority of old people fit the stereotype. Bernard (1974: 13) advises that comparisons of two groups which include much variability, such as all men and all women, should be worded carefully to preserve rather than hide diversity. Here, the statement that old people are not as healthy as younger people hides the variability, while the statement that more old people than young people have poor health preserves the diversity. The probability of being ill is greater for persons 65 and over, but it is less than 100%. How much less will be discussed below.

Only in the last twenty-five years has an attempt been made to separate the physical effects of age and disease (Birren et al., 1963), and whether biological aging per se causes physical decline or whether the decline is caused by the presence of disease is now being addressed in research (Masoro, 1972; Doyle, 1972). Butler (1968: 235) concludes in a summary of a multidisciplinary study designed to "disentangle the contributions of disease, social losses, preexisting personality, and the like from changes that might more properly be regarded as age-specific," that these separate factors account for a great deal of what is thought to be "naturally" caused by aging per se.

In confronting the assumption that modifying old with unhealthy is redundant, the most immediate roadblock is the difficulty of defining good health and ill health. The World Health Organization rejects the definition of good health as absence of disease or infirmity, in favor of a positive definition that incorporates physical, mental, and social well-being as criteria (Confrey and Goldstein, 1960). Needless to say, except in blatant cases of "unwell-being," assessing someone's health using this definition is difficult. Even if the negative definition is used, that is, defining "unhealthy" as the presence of disease or infirmity, the decision to place someone in the category "unhealthy" may depend on extensive tests that are rarely made, in part, because they are costly, time-consuming, and difficult to interpret (Butler, 1968), and in part because doctors often consider the old unworthy recipients of their valuable time (Coombs and Goldman, 1972; Sudnow, 1967). The old also tend to interpret physical discomfort as signs of aging and, therefore, not important enough to indicate consultation with a physician (Shanas, 1962: 49-52).

A physical examination by a doctor, however, is rarely used as the criteria for categorizing respondents as healthy or unhealthy in social research, or even in collecting morbidity data (Confrey and Goldstein, 1960: 167). More commonly used are reports of health status of household members by heads of household, or, for specific age groups, by the respondents themselves. Shanas (1962: 188) constructed an index of illness "based on answers to questions about illness, health problems and time spent in bed or in a wheelchair because of sickness." Of the 1,734 persons constituting Shanas's random sample of noninstitutionalized persons aged 65 and over, only 10% were classified as "very sick." Forty-six percent had no or minor health complaints. Forty-four percent had a few more health complaints, but these were generally not considered to be physically incapacitating. These findings are much different from the belief of most people in the United States that "old age and ill health are synonymous" (Shanas, 1962: 180).

An increasingly popular and much more socially meaningful method of assessing health is focused on the consequences of physical problems. Townsend (1963) developed an "index of incapacity" based on the assumption that an old person living alone must be able to perform certain tasks in order to maintain independence. This index was used in a large cross-cultural study of noninstitutionalized old persons (Shanas et al., 1968: 27).

The index requires an answer to six questions from the old person: (1) Can he go out-of-doors? (2) Can he walk up and down stairs? (3) Can he get about the house? (4) Can he wash and bathe himself? (5) Can he dress himself and put on shoes? (6) Can he cut his own toenails? The old person is asked whether he can do each of these tasks without difficulty and without assistance, with some difficulty but still without the help of another person, and finally, with difficulty and only with the help of another person. . . . Scores on the index of incapacity may range from zero to 12. The ability to perform a task without any restriction is assigned a score of zero, the ability to perform a task only with difficulty is assigned a score of one, and complete inability to perform a task is assigned a score of two.

In the United States sample, 63% of persons aged 65 and over had no difficulty performing these tasks. Twenty-two percent had scores of 1 or 2, leaving only 15% with scores of 3 or more. Inability to perform any of the activities used for the index is not automatically incapacitating. Not all old people live in physical environments where climbing stairs is necessary, although environments without stairs are probably scarce. A helpful spouse may make difficulty in dressing a minor inconvenience. These examples point to the importance of the environmental and social context within which persons, regardless of age, fail to develop or lose abilities to perform certain tasks.

All of the above measures of health, varied though they are, contradict the assumption that poor health and advanced years are synonymous. This finding cannot be over emphasized, for it is this assumption that is most detrimental to the social and self identities of the aged. Problems associated with aging are seen as lying within the individual, as physical and mental deterioration, rather than as located in social arrangements. To illustrate the far-ranging effects of the assumption, an advertisement that is now included in each issue of *The Gerontologist* is helpful. The three page colored advertisement pictures a disheveled old woman who illustrates the proper patient for Hydergene, a drug to use "when the symptoms are clear, but the cause is not." The drug is billed as "a frequently effective agent for 'gray area' symptoms in the elderly patient." Confusion, lack of self-care, dizziness, mood-depression, and unsociability qualify as "gray areas." A description of the latter is revealing.

> In the elderly, unsociability can range from bursts of anger and hostility to withdrawal from interpersonal relationships. While social and economic displacement may contribute to her attitudes, there may also be physiologic aspects to the problem [The Gerontologist, 1976: 107].

Behavioral responses to a personally damaging socially defined situation are seen as medical symptoms, rather than as legitimate means of expressing dissatisfaction with an intolerable situation. This is the now familiar paradox of "blaming the victim" (Ryan, 1971).

That human bodies undergo biological changes as the years since birth accumulate cannot be denied. These changes are socially evaluated and are seen, for the most part, as negative: wrinkles are ugly while smooth skin is beautiful. Thinking and speaking rapidly is admirable while accumulated knowledge that makes rapid verbal judgments difficult is not. These negative evaluations are matters of social definition and are often summarized in the simple phrase "youth-oriented society." As with many simple phrases, this one fails to express the diverse ramifications and meanings to social actors of a complex, socially constructed belief system.

Summary

This chapter is intended to accomplish two ends. First, the argument has been made that old age is a socially constructed category. The stereotypical old person is impoverished, socially isolated, and physically disabled, and at least in part, this is an accurate depiction. However, the accuracy stems not from the effects of the accumulation of years per se, but from current social arrangements, especially economic ones, that have placed the aged in a marginal position in relation to the ongoing social order. Second, the accuracy of the stereotype has been reviewed and found wanting. The aged, and especially aged widows, have a great probability of being impoverished and of being socially isolated, although research on the extended family has revealed at least more structural support than was once thought to exist. The depiction of the aged as decrepit and unhealthy has been challenged and isolated as the most important misconception. Imputed ill health is used to justify the current position of the aged in society, thereby placing responsibility on the old themselves rather than on social arrangements that place them in a marginal and demeaned position.

NOTES

1. Cross-cultural evidence for the assertion that oldness is socially constructed is missing from this analysis because who is defined as old is not considered problematic by anthropologists. The taken-for-granted defining of persons as old is clear in Simmons's (1945) catalogue of findings about old people in 71 tribes using 109 variables for describing tribes and 56 variables for describing participation and treatment of the aged for each sex. Who in each tribe was old was a matter of each anthropologist's (informed) opinion. Some used physical infirmity as a criterion. Some used social position. Some used chronological age. Some used appearance. Most used convoluted combinations that appears to be based in Western thought. Although the catalogue and correlations are interesting, a reader whose focus is on social definitions of old is left with more questions than answers. For a similar critique of cross-cultural research on gender see Kessler and McKenna (1978: 21-41).

2. Statements such as the following are questionable in light of the unavailability to women of partners of the opposite sex. "Perhaps the most damaging to the self-image of the person grown older is the false idea that sex dies when the retirement age comes. If the wish is father to the child, the belief is also often parent to the action (or inaction)" (Smith, 1973). Perhaps a belief in the necessity to express sexuality in a social world in which the chances to act are nonexistent will father (or mother) a self-image that is even more damaged.

3. An interesting consequence of the increasing financial ability of the aged to maintain homes of their own is an increase in

the number of old people enumerated as "poor" in our surveys of low-income families. The reason: squeezed to the wall financially, many aged Americans have been forced to double up with their working children or other relatives and have thereby been counted as above the poverty line, along with the family on which they were reluctantly dependent. When such dependent aged receive even small increases in real social security benefits, they move out on their own, choosing a more independent life [Wilensky, 1975: 91].

Chapter 3

SELF-IDENTITY: OLDNESS IS A STIGMA

The stage has now been set for a consideration of aged social actors and the methods they employ to cope with occupying a devalued status. In turning to the perspective of individuals who must cope on an everyday level with being old, the most salient feature is uncertainty. The social worlds in which old women pursue their daily rounds are fraught with uncertainty, perhaps most obviously because of their close proximity to death. The overriding source of uncertainty, however, is related to self-identity. The lack of a rite of passage that places people in the age category "old" and the lack of norms and expectations that prescribe "old" behavior in American society combine to place old persons in ambiguous social positions: how are they to view themselves in relation to their age? Old is a stigma, "an attribute that is deeply discrediting" (Goffman, 1963: 3), but because of these absences it is a "weak" stigma. These factors combine to make self-identity, the way in which the old woman views herself, problematic. Evidence to support these assertions will be presented in the following pages.

Difficulty of Applying the Label

There is no clear consensus on when a member of society becomes old, no line across which the middle-aged pass to become socially old, no specific graduation ceremony. There are events that mark changes in status: retirement dinners accompanied by the presentation of the proverbial gold watch, the first social security check, the first grandchild or great grandchild, and these may be noted jokingly or with alarm. They do not, however, change the actor's social identity from middle-aged to old.

The difficulties of deciding who is old must be confronted by research gerontologists and those who design social services for the elderly. The criterion for inclusion in the category is usually set at an arbitrary lower age limit ranging from 55 to 70, and, once made, rarely comes under scrutiny. Locally funded social service agencies probably choose the lowest age limits because it is to their advantage to include as many members of the area as possible in their target population in order to justify budgets. The high minimum age limit of 70 for this research was chosen in order to insure agreement that the informants are, indeed, old. Thus, definitions of "old" are not made on a societal level by general consensus, but depend on the purpose of the definer.

More recently, there has been recognition of the heterogeneity of "the elderly," and new categories are gaining popularity in the social gerontological literature; for example, the "young old" and the "old old," and the "well elderly" and the "frail elderly." In the presentation of data in this analysis, the informants are referred to categorically as "old women" to emphasize "old" rather than chronological age. Chronological age is not a reliable predictor of an individual's social behavior or physical condition. Referring to the age of the informants would only perpetuate the myth, shared by the old with younger members of society, that knowing an individual's year of birth supplies information on which to base concrete beliefs and expectations about that person. All of the informants are over sixty-five, most are over seventy, and many are over eighty years of age.

Those who are arbitrarily defined as old may not feel comfortable with the designation. The following comment from a recipient of a questionnaire sent to "senior citizens" indicates the problem:

> Why include 50 year old people when many are employed and many in M _____ are professors at the University? All of a sudden I feel 150 years old!

A number of women who supplied data for this research advised that they were poor informants because they really were not old yet. Many members of society claim that they do not use chronological age as their everyday definition of old, but instead use physical condition and level of energy as overriding considerations for applying the label. There is also evidence that old people who are personally known to respondents are considered atypical old people, in better condition than most of their age contemporaries (Shanas, 1962). Lack of agreement on who qualifies as old, then, contributes to uncertainty in the social world.

In addition, there are few norms and expectations governing "old" behavior. Although it is still popular to view old age as a social role, and Burgess (1960) is criticized for describing the aged as trapped in a "roleless role," Rosow (1974) has made a convincing argument that there is no specific role available into which the aged may be socialized. There is no role content, no norms that prescribe "old" behavior. Values and norms that are applicable in middle-age do not disappear. "Act your age" may be a command that children and adolescents can heed, but once adulthood is achieved, "acting your age" is taken-for-granted. Being an adult is an ascribed status, and adults are not rewarded for acting like adults, although they risk being labeled as less than persons, or even "nonpersons," if they fail to meet expectations (Sarbin, 1968).

A recent critique of the "roleless role" assertion shows the poverty of the conception of retirement as a role, and, by implication, of old age as a role. Atchley (1976) argues that "retiree" is a role in the same way that "alumnus" is a role. Except for those actively involved in alumni associations, however, "alumnus" is a label, not a role. "Retired" and "old" are also labels that fail to prescribe behavior or relationships and, therefore, are not roles. The norms and expectations that Atchley lists for the retired, living independently within their incomes, are applicable to all adults. Adults who fail to perform these minimal requirements may legitimately be treated as nonpersons, and this is precisely the danger that the aged confront.

To summarize: although old is considered a legitimate social category and label, it is not clear who belongs in the category or who can be labeled "old." Except for a few obvious correlates of old age, such as collecting pensions and social security, there are a few behavioral prescriptions that apply specifically to the aged and not to adults generally. At the same time, however, age is an attribute that has social meanings and is taken into account in social interaction.

Spoiled Identity

Appearance establishes identifications and chronological age is an important component of appearance. "By appearing, a person *announces* his identity, *shows* his value, *expresses* his mood, and *proposes* his attitude" (Stone, 1975: 87), but only if his or her appearance can be fairly easily interpreted. The behavioral correlates of wrinkles, gray hair, and other appearential aspects of oldness are not easily identified, and, thus, ambiguity is introduced into both the social identity and the self-identity of the old person.

That old is a demeaning status is easily documented in this youth-oriented society (Simon, 1968). Old people are the possessors of a stigma that is in a middle ground between discrediting and discreditable. Old age is a stigma in the sense that Goffman (1963) uses it, but it is a stigma with a few peculiarities. This is due in great part to the fact that most people will be old someday, so that regarding old people as "not quite human" is not as comfortable as regarding people with one leg as "not quite human." It is "not normal" to lose a leg, but it is "normal" to grow old.

In his discussion of the attitudes of "we normals" toward persons with stigmas, Goffman points out five fairly distinct ways in which discrimination—that has the effect of limiting the stigmatized individual's life chances—occurs.

We construct a stigma-theory, an ideology to explain his inferiority and account for the danger he represents, sometimes rationalizing an animosity based on other differences, such as those of social class. We use specific stigma terms such as cripple, bastard, moron in our daily discourse as a source of metaphor and imagery, typically without giving thought to the original meaning. We tend to impute a wide range of imperfections on the basis of the original one, and at the same time impute some desirable but undesired attributes, often of a supernatural cast, such as "sixth sense," or "understanding." . . . Further, we may perceive his defensive response to his situation as a direct expression of his defect (Goffman, 1963: 5-6).

All of these are applicable to old people.

As was noted in the previous chapter, old people are assumed by virtue of their age to be physically, and, therefore, mentally incapacitated. The stigma theory that age and poor health are synonymous is used to justify a mandatory retirement age, but it also has an effect on everyday interaction. Old people because of their advanced age are more

easily assumed to be incapable of performing adequately as
adult members of society as the following excerpt from a
newspaper article illustrates.

> The little lady must have been nearly seventy years old. The gray
> suit she was wearing was obviously her Good Suit and her smile
> was the kind older ladies always wear when it's a sparkling San
> Francisco day and they're on their way to meet a friend for
> lunch. Her straw hat was topped with dollops of red lacquered
> cherries and clusters of shining angelica. In a movie, only Shirley
> Booth could have played her role. Pausing at the curb, she looked
> both ways, then nodded to herself the way a child nods when
> rules have been properly acknowledged [San Francisco-Chronicle-
> Examiner, 1973].[1]

The picture the reader has is of a shadow, a person who is no
longer a fully participating member of society, who no longer
has the interest or the capacity to relate more than marginally to the world around her, and this is, "of course," due to
advanced age.

Specific stigma terms are found in popular epithets such as
"dirty old man," "old maid," "old geezer," "old wive's tale,"
"old fogey," and newspaper articles such as the following.

> Sunday concerts of the Sacramento Symphony are Little Old
> Lady matinees: Scores of L.O.L.'s in their cloth coats with fur
> collars, tottering in pairs to their seats. It's not that there aren't
> plenty of students and other people in the audience—just that the
> L.O.L.'s seem to be the most noticeable element. Fortunately,
> the concert on Sunday, January 14, did not reflect the rather
> stodgy tastes of L.O.L.'s. [California Aggie, 1973].

The wide range of imperfections imputed to accompany
the accumulation of years on earth have come under scrutiny
in studies of the attitudes of various groups toward old
people (Drake, 1957; McTavish, 1971; Tuckman and Lorge,
1953). One of these imperfections is "senility," used to refer
to various forms of social incompetence. The following letter

to "Dear Abby" is indicative (San Francisco Chronicle, 1973):

> Dear Abby—I had a very irritating experience recently at a family gathering. One of my aunts greeted me with, "I didn't recognize you because you got so fat!" (And she said this in front of a lot of people.)
>
> As one who has always been heavy, I am very sensitive about my weight and I found this very embarrassing. I feel that such comments are as rude and uncalled for as making fun of a cripple or an otherwise handicapped person.
>
> My family tells me to drop the matter because my aunt is elderly and should be excused. I maintain that age is no excuse. What is your opinion? BURNED[2]

There is some question, then, of whether or not old people should be excused from following the rules of interaction that "normal" adults are expected to follow. Another imperfection is illustrated in the following joke about an old man recounted by Sam Ervin.

> A gentleman, who was rather prominent in his community attained his 95th birthday anniversary. On that day the newspaper reporters came around to interview him. And one of them asked how old he was. He said, "This is my 95th birthday anniversary."
>
> And the reporter said, "Well, you have lived a long, long time and have seen many changes in your life."
>
> And he said, "Yes, and I was against every one of them" [Los Angeles Times, 1973].

This joke not only points to the imputed conservativeness that the old supposedly possess, but also to the imputed inability of the young and old to communicate because there have been so many changes, both technological and social, in this century that there is no basis for communication.

The "desirable but undesired attribute" that is imputed to accompany aging is "wisdom that can be acquired only through living;" something old people have managed to do more of than younger members of society. Unfortunately, their wisdom is considered outdated and is, therefore, discounted.

> One item that is on the agenda is UC President Charles Hitch's plan to woo aging faculty members into early retirement. Hitch would allow tenured professors who are 60 years of age and have 20 or more years of university experience to retire at reduced benefits.
>
> The move is Hitch's answer to a growing problem at UC campus-wide: A growing generation gap between an older faculty and younger student body, and a lack of opportunities for assistant professors.
>
> (UC Davis, except in agriculture and veterinary medical fields, does not face the problem of Berkeley and UCLA with an aging, entrenched faculty. Hitch has, however, ordered a study of faculty age distribution on all nine campuses. [Woodland Daily Democrat, 1973]

Thus, even in an area such as higher education, where the amount and value of professors' knowledge would seem to increase with each passing year and, thereby, increase their value to students and to their disciplines, advanced years is a liability.

The last way in which "we normals" discriminate is perhaps the most devastating for it requires that the old take care lest their responses to a personally threatening social definition be labeled as further evidence of their incompetence. The advertisement noted above for the drug to use for "gray area" symptoms indicates this danger as does the following remark made by one of the informants.

> If there is some little thing, they just take it for granted that she is getting old. I think people do that with most older people. They seem to consider she's old and she may not mean all she does or says.[3]

The material recounted here, then, suggests that oldness spoils identity. At the same time "old" is a peculiar stigma in that which members of society are also members of the category "old" is unclear.

Weak Stigma

In his discussion of the variety of attributes that can be stigmatizing, Goffman (1963) emphasizes that the effect of a given attribute on interaction varies with situational circumstances, that in reality a stigma is a relationship, not an attribute at all. Unfortunately, any discussion of a specific attribute makes it appear concrete and hides its dependence on the meaning derived from the situation. By choosing as his examples attributes that by general consensus are stigmatizing, i.e., blindness, facial deformities, speech impediments, mental hospitalization, he detracts somewhat from emphasis on situational dependency. To some extent, his discussion of back, civil, and out-of-bounds places points to the variety of social meanings that an attribute may have. It is this variety of social meanings that is important in viewing oldness as a "weak" stigma.

Ascribed characteristics usually serve as "background variables": they affect interaction but are generally unnoticed unless they are glaringly out of the ordinary. A person's appearance, including gender and age, is taken into account with little conscious thought about its social meaning, although its meaning is very important for the ensuing interaction. Old age, however, is not so easily relegated to the status of a background variable.

Travisano (1970) presents a schema, drawing on Banton (1965), for analyzing the centrality of a particular identity, centrality being defined in terms of the number of situations in which the identity is dominant. He sees age and gender as basic identities in that they function most often to help set the ground rules for interaction in terms of language and demeanor. . . . They are neither central nor secondary to interaction, rather they are woven throughout it generally without much ado [Travisano, 1970: 604].

Between basic identities and independent identities, the two ends of the continuum, lie general identities. A general identity has

the quality of a basic identity, i.e., it determines the language and demeanor. It is not a basic identity, however, because it tends to be central to interaction: it is the identity around which the interaction turns [Travisano, 1970: 604].

For an old person, age moves from the end of this continuum toward the middle in that it is no longer clear whether age is a background variable, that is, a basic identity, or the one on which interaction should focus, that is, a general identity.

In a sense, then, the old are "midstream between danger and discovery" (Strauss, 1959: 38), in that they are unsure of how to view themselves in relation to their chronological age. And those with whom they interact suffer from the same uncertainty, for it is not always clear whether age is a major attribute to which to attend or if some other status attribute should take priority. This is the requirement of a "weak" stigma:

once a person with a particular stigma attains high occupational, political, or financial position . . . a new career is likely to be thrust upon him, that of representing his category. . . . (The weakness of a stigma can thus be measured by how eminent a member of the category may be and yet manage to avoid these pressures) [Goffman, 1963: 26-27].

Thus, when the president promotes or vetoes legislation for the elderly, no one suggests that he is acting in his own self-interest as a member of the category old. However, persons of the same age who put in their own sewer system

("Elderly Residents Bypass the Bureaucracy"), or who are swindled ("Older Man Bilked of Home, Money"), or who for some other reason are newsworthy but lack an important social position that identifies them, are considered by the media to be instances of the category.

Whether or not age is to be considered the salient dimension of an old person's social identity, is not always clear, and, indeed, is uncertain for both the possessor of the attribute and those she or he meets. The old, then, have a great deal of latitude to decide what old is and whether or not they personally fit the definition.

Shared Definitions

Old people share with other members of society the stereotypical view of old people. They have certainly been members of society long enough to have been socialized into a "normal" point of view, and the moral career of the stigmatized includes this important first step.

> One phase of this socialization process is that through which the stigmatized person learns and incorporates the standpoint of the normal, acquiring thereby the identity beliefs of the wider society and a general idea of what it would be like to possess a particular stigma [Goffman, 1963: 32].

Comments by informants indicate they have, indeed, been well socialized. An old man explained the root of the problems at the Senior Citizens' Center.

> I think you'll find that as people get older they get more set in their ways. They are not used to having their families cross them and they are used to having authority. I think you'll find that down at the Center.

Problems at the Senior Center, then, according to this man, are due to the age of the participants, rather than to the difficulties inherent in attempting to organize the activities of any large group of adults.

One informant pointed out that she gets along better with young people because "they probably think better than women my own age." This is revealing because it points to a dilemma created by belief in the stereotype. This old woman, in internalizing the stereotype, rejects old women as worthy friends at the same time that young people who have also internalized the stereotype and, seeing her as old and therefore unworthy, reject her as a possible friend. The logical consequence of this is social isolation.

Another old man, and this one a likely recruit for the Gray Panthers, who might, therefore, be expected to see the ageist nature of his comments, referred to a job that he felt was not suited for old people because it requires "a lot of patience. Someone who was older wouldn't be able to put up with Mable. They'd tell her where to get off. I think that's a really taxing job," and therefore, not suitable for "impatient old people." Still another example is found in one woman's reference to sportscaster, Ira Blue, then in his seventies. "He's not what he used to be. He's getting into our age bracket, too, you know."

All these data point to the internalization by old people of the stereotype and the assumption that there is something about old people by virtue of their age that makes them members of a legitimate social category. These "somethings" are all undesirable attributes.

Summary

Old age is not a social category with a simple definition or an obvious membership. It is a social category with negative connotations, but, because of the ambiguity surrounding membership, to whom negative attributes may be imputed, is unclear. Oldness is a stigma, but a weak one, so that the second phase of the moral career of a stigmatized person, that is, learning that s/he "possesses a particular stigma and, this time in detail, the consequences of possessing it" (Goffman, 1963: 32), may be avoided, or at least softened, as the following chapter will make clear. However, old people have successfully navigated the first phase of the moral career; they have internalized the "normal" point of view about old age.

NOTES

1. Although this example and the following examples from the mass media may not be considered data by some, they are characteristic of the "folk wisdom" of the culture. They are demeaning statements about a category of persons, the old, that can be made without thought to the stereotypes they perpetuate. Similar statements about other groups, especially blacks and ethnic minorities and, more recently, women, are no longer common, except in newspapers that make no claim to being unbiased.

2. Abby agrees that "age could be an excuse," but advises Burned to lose weight. Obesity is also a stigma, and since neither party is "normal," neither is blameless.

3. Unless credit is attributed to another source, quoted passages are from interviews and field observations.

Chapter 4

MAINTAINING A PRECARIOUS SELF-IDENTITY

This chapter will focus on how persons with weak stigmas, in this case old women, maintain their images of themselves. The ambiguity involved in applying the label "old" gives old women some latitude in defining themselves as "old" or "not old." As was pointed out above, oldness is not a pivotal self-identity for most old people: old women in most situations reject the label old for themselves, even though they use it to describe others who are age peers. However, it is a pivotal social identity, one that others impute to the old woman, in those situations in which another of her status attributes is not more salient.

Numerous studies have focused on the "adjustment patterns" of those who accept and those who reject the label old for themselves (Brubaker and Powers, 1976; Kastenbaum and Durkee, 1963). Generally, findings indicate that under some conditions adopting the label is indicative of a "good adjustment" to old age (Phillips, 1957). Research has also been directed toward finding correlates of a self-definition of old, including widowhood, retirement, physical impairment, and others who think of the person as old, all of which have been shown to affect likelihood of describing oneself as old (Atchley, 1972; Blau, 1956; Preston, 1968). There is some question, however, about the everyday meaning of a response to this forced-choice question. The situation of being confronted by an interviewer and being asked to identify oneself as young, middle-aged, old, or elderly, is atypical, and responses in this situation may not spill over into daily round situations (Deutscher, 1973).

Others have focused on the political implications of the refusal of the aged to embrace the label "old," and within the field of social gerontology there is an ongoing debate concerning the validity of viewing the aged as an active or even a potential political interest group (Binstock, 1972; Rose, 1965). Maggie Kuhn, founder and leader of the Gray Panthers, attempts to "raise consciousness" and recruit politically oriented members by inviting listeners to follow her example and publicly proclaim that they are old and proud to be old. Although the membership of the Gray Panthers is growing, it is telling that a substantial portion of the members are not old themselves, but professionals concerned with the welfare of the aged.

The issues addressed here, however, are not related to adjustment or politics but to self-identity. Even though an old woman may not think of herself as old, she must deal with others in a variety of situations who do think of her as old. In addition, having internalized the stereotypes that author negative expectations of old behavior, she may find evidence in her own behavior that she is, after all, an old woman. The strategies for protecting her image of herself in these two situations, that is, those situations in which she interacts with others who assume she is an old woman and those in which she recognizes indications in her own thoughts and actions that she may be an old woman after all, will be addressed here.

Lofland (1976: 100) has pointed out that:

> All encounters involve people in immediate interaction, but not all interactants need be in separate bodies. . . . To the degree that people engage in internal dialogues with themselves, we may speak of self-encounters, or in the context of situation and strategy analysis, self-management encounters.

The delineation of strategies here, then, are divided somewhat arbitrarily between encounters with others and encounters with self.

Encounters with Others

Even though the old woman does not think of herself as old, she must deal with situations in which other people think she is old. In conversations with others, especially younger others, the old woman is faced with the assumption on the listener's part that she is an instance of the category "old woman." She must explain to people who assume she is an old woman that she is not. Thus, when an old woman is talking about old people in general she is careful to point out that she does not consider herself old. The observation that old women use one definition of old for themselves and another for age peers is closely paralleled in Rosow's (1967) research. He found that 50% of his sample described themselves as middle-aged, while at the same time 85% agreed that old people who felt middle-aged were simply deluding themselves.

One old woman who was a retired nurse and had worked with hospitalized old people said, "I just loved those old people. (pause) But see, I don't consider myself in that category." Another woman realizing that the person to whom she was speaking would need an explanation for why she excluded herself from the category "elderly," supplied one.

> I have seen so many elderly women (I don't know whether they were older than I, but some people age faster than others), and some of them could hardly walk, you know.

She does not think of herself as one of "the elderly," in this case, because she does not meet her situational criterion for being included, "unable to walk."

In managing encounters with others who may assume that they are "just old women," the informants used four strategies.

Suppress Evidence

One simple strategy an old woman may use is to avoid telling her age. As one informant said, "I never tell them how old I am. I just tell them I'm old enough." A woman aged eighty-plus recounted an experience at the Senior Citizens' Center that had occurred the previous day:

> They said, "Poor soul, she's in her eighties." I just laughed. They never count me. The lady yesterday was only seventy.

Another woman confided:

> I don't think they know my age. I don't ask them theirs. People don't think I'm as old as I am, so I don't go around blabbin' it.

Thus, she avoids confronting publicly the significance of her age. Of course, for some old women this strategy is not available. One informant stated, "I've always looked older than my age. I've sort of gotten used to it. You probably think I'm older than I am."

This strategy falls under the generic heading of "information management," a tactic available to persons with nonvisible discrediting attributes (Goffman, 1963). Chronological age is assumed to be visible and this strategy, logically, would not appear to be available to the old. However, most members of society have such strong beliefs that physical incapacity and old age are highly correlated that when an old person's age is mentioned many persons are completely surprised. For many old women, then, suppressing evidence is a successful strategy.

Different Definitions of Old

The old woman may have a definition of old that is based on criteria other than chronological age. The strategy follows logically since, as was noted above, old women have internalized societal definitions of old and at the same time view themselves personally as not belonging to the category. Slightly simplified, what occurs is that the old woman has one_definition for other old people and one for herself. With this in mind, remarks such as the following take on meaning: "I don't think I ever got old. That's all there is to it. And I never will be. If I live to be one hundred, I'm not going to be old."

To make clear that she does not consider herself old, she may share her definitions that "It's what's inside that counts." As one old woman said:

In the old vintage, eighty was the little black bonnet affair and that sort of thing. I don't think we should think of age chronologically at all. It's your outlook more than anything else.

Another old woman showed the interviewer a pamphlet entitled, "How to Stay Young Forever,"

and I read this. Now if you practice this, you will be taking on the qualities associated with youth. People will never think about your age. They'll just think how young you are.

This is an overstatement of the point and very few of the old women would agree with so strong a proclamation, but many believe in the basic philosophy. Two other examples of old people's beliefs that they are young by virtue of what is inside are found in the following.

> I don't feel like I'm seventy-two. I'm surprised when I look in the mirror. I went down to get my hair cut the other day and I'm always surprised when I look down and see all that gray hair, because I don't feel gray-headed.
>
> Being old is like playing a character role. Inside you're just the same. But you have a lot of stuff clamped onto you. Various ailments. They won't kill me yet, but they're no joke. You can't walk twenty miles. You're just the same inside. You are doing a character part [J. B. Priestly, San Francisco Chronicle-Examiner, 1974].

Thus, each old person considers herself to be just an ordinary person and forgets whenever possible that she has the trappings of oldness. But when she must attend to the trappings, she explains that she is not what she seems. This strategy, more than the others, falls under both encounters with others and encounters with self.

Bring in Outside Sources

To increase the credibility of her belief in her "not oldness," she may bring in outside sources to say, in effect, "Other reputable people do not think of me as old."

> I think I'm pretty spry for my age. I'm only 83. I just had a birthday last Friday. People tell me I get along just fine.
>
> They don't treat me like I'm a helpless old lady. I thank God I'm as good as I am. Very few think of me as old as I am. They don't. People can't tell how old I am.

This strategy shows clearly the uncertainty with which the old woman views herself. She feels that her word alone is not sufficient proof and that, by citing others who think of her as not old or treat her as not old, she will somehow be more convincing to dubious listeners.

Avoid Threatening Situations

Avoiding situations in which her oldness may be the pivotal or general identity is one way to maintain a self-identity of "not old." She may do this by organizing her daily activities so that she is never in such a situation. As one woman stated,

> You know about young people, but I don't pay any attention to them. Go over here to K-Mart and they take up the whole sidewalk. And the way they look at you, they wouldn't get off that sidewalk. You have to go around them. . . . I don't like to go over there on Saturday or even late Friday afternoon because school's out.

This old woman can purposely avoid those potentially demeaning situations by doing her shopping during school hours. Another example which is less clear on the surface is: "I don't hear so I don't go to church. I listen to a service on TV." This seems like an adequate explanation if it is assumed that the only reason people attend church services is to hear a sermon, but the statement loses credence when the many social functions of the weekly gathering are considered. A more accurate statement might be: "I don't go to church because I can't participate in the stated reason for being there and that makes me very aware of my oldness."

Another form this strategy may take is to plan ahead to avoid doing things that others may think are a reflection of advanced age and thereby diminish credibility. On one occasion at a senior citizens center, a woman viewed the beginning of a downpour with some dismay. She had brought her raincoat, but had left it in the car. "I thought you'd laugh at me if I brought it in, old grandma with her raincoat and her boots." Thinking about her granddaughter's wedding that was to take place in the near future, one old woman described her nervousness:

> Of course I sort of get anxious and worried about whether I dress right or look right or not or whether I say the things I should say or shouldn't say, and, you know, sometimes you forget if you've got more information that you're supposed to.

Everyone may feel a tinge of anxiety before a formal occasion, but old people fear that a social faux pas will be viewed as an indication of senility. By taking special care to see that her props and conversations are correct, the old woman acts to protect her self-image.

The safest way to avoid potentially problematic situations is perhaps the most general, and that is simply to avoid verbal and nonverbal interaction, especially with young people, who are seen as the least sympathetic. As one woman put it:

> I mix with my own age. I don't feel at home with younger people. They're nice and I love them and I love to watch them enjoy themselves, but I don't mix with them. I'm a wet blanket at my age on their activities. So I don't want to spoil anyone's fun. I like my own age. I feel at home there.

Tales of what happens when encounters take place are fairly rare, perhaps because the old women manage their daily rounds so well that encounters themselves are rare. One such incident is reported to her peers by an old woman.

> I was walking home from shopping. I guess it was Thursday. And there was this young fella, see, and his friend. I was carrying my groceries. They were heavy. And I was walking, you know, kind of slow. And that young fella called, "Why aren't you in your grave?" He and his friend laughed. [Hochschild, 1969: 165].

Another old woman recounted a similar incident. On her way to the grocery store, she had passed a group of small children, and I grinned at them because I like children, and one of them looked up and she said, "You're ugly, ugly, ugly." And I said, "Well, so are you." And one of them was going to hit me with a stick. I said, "If you do, I'll call the sheriff." . . . I was surprised to death. I must have had a long face because I didn't feel very good and it takes all of me to get there and all of me to get back. But I have to laugh about it now.

The highway is another public place where the old meet the young.

There have been a few occasions with younger people. Well, when I say younger I don't mean in the middle twenties, I mean in the teens. I had the feeling they were saying, "The poor old soul," especially when I used to drive a car. They had the attitude, the look on their face, "What the devil are you doing out in a car? You belong home in a rocking chair." But I can truly say it wasn't very often. But I'm kind of stupid. It might be that I didn't even notice.

The most frequent examples are of interaction with grand-children.

I would try to tell these kids what we used to do when I was their age. "Oh, Grandma, they don't do that anymore. They don't do that anymore."

The safest adaptation to having what she says dismissed as irrelevant and outdated, a severe hardship to her self-identity, is simply to quit talking, not to put herself on the line. A conversation between two old women indicates that this is not uncommon.

Goldie had helped her granddaughter find a job. The grand-daughter was surprised that Goldie's advice had been valid. Ellen said that she didn't like to give her children or grandchildren advice. They think she doesn't know what she's talking about because times have changed so much. She just doesn't bother any more to tell them what she thinks.

The risks involved in conversing with younger people, and even in encountering them in public settings, are often too great to warrant putting herself in such situations.

Disengagement theory is one explanation of this type of data. Cumming and Henry (1961: 14) write:

> the old person is less involved in the life around him than he was when he was younger.... Aging is an inevitable mutual with-drawal resulting in decreased interaction between the aging person and others in the social system he belongs to.

The data presented here indicate that lack of interaction is not mutually rewarding, but a response to a situation that is threatening to the old woman's self-identity.

Encounters with Self

In encounters with self, the old woman must deal with signs, both physical and social, which indicate that she is a "typical" old woman after all. Again, some of these strategies might also be considered encounters with others, but, for the most part, are strategies for coping with self-doubt rather than directly with the doubts of others.

What Seems Like Oldness Really Isn't

Occasionally the old woman recognizes things about herself that she associates with oldness, but she is quick to find other explanations.

> I used to be able to watch television. Now I fall asleep in the middle of the darn show. ... But my son-in-law, Bob, he's half my age, and he falls asleep.

> They just can't realize that maybe it's swell for you, but if it's swell for you and cutting someone else's throat, what good is it? And I'm not just talking because it's almost over. I have always felt that way. I don't think I've changed in my philosophy or my

ideals in life anymore than when I was fourteen years old and I still maintain that you can't have it all unless you're going to hurt someone else.

One old woman has noticed in the last year that she does not like to be with large groups of noisy people.

Now that may be my age. I think that perhaps being older, I can't tolerate it as well. That's being honest. And I think, too, the world is really noisier.

As these episodes indicate, doubt may rear its ugly head, but age is soon dismissed as the "real" cause of her behavior and her beliefs.

Attach New Meaning to Old Activities

One of the features noted above of growing old in American society is the attenuation that occurs in the number of bonds to other people. The social-structural facts of oldness include a reduction in the number of roles available to old people. Old people are retired and widowed and independent, which is a euphemistic way of saying they live alone. They are still parents and grandparents and siblings, but these roles have no particular content. They are weak ways of identifying oneself. The old widow, in losing important roles, has fewer ways of viewing herself. She can no longer identify herself as a nurse, for example, or the postman's wife, or even the retired postman's wife. Being retired or widowed are identities that are nonrelationships, and the roles that do relate to other people lack content (Rosow, 1974) and cannot be used to justify existence.

That justification for existence is important to old people can be seen in the extreme in this letter to Abby (San Francisco Chronicle-Examiner, 1973).

Dear Abby—You asked to hear from senior citizens: Would that some compassionate, benevolent God take this body and accept

the soul of man on the day he voluntarily retires or is arbitrarily
retired from his work and soon becomes . . . Useless Seventy

This occurs in less dramatic forms in old peoples' daily lives.
For example, when I asked an old woman what she had been
doing since I last saw her, she replied, "Nothing much," and
after a slight pause, "But I've been active." This old woman is
in all likelihood doing the same things she has always done—
cooking, cleaning, marketing, watching television, visiting
with friends—but she is no longer doing these things for
anyone, and therefore has no estimable labels for what she is
doing, no way to justify her existence to me or to herself.
This is not totally situational. Even in "age dense" housing,
this need to justify exists among age peers. Hochschild
(1973) found that the women in the housing project she
studied regarded their "downstairs activities" (making things
for others or for money) as work and were suspicious of
those who stayed upstairs and did not join them. Justification even between age peers would appear to be important,
although acceptable justifications may be more easily negotiated among age peers.

The lack of justifying labels for herself, then, is a problem
that is dealt with in two ways. One, illustrated above by
"Useless Seventy," is to personally accept, sometimes bitterly, the stereotypical denotation of the old as worthless to
society. This stance is not typical of the informants.
Attaching new meaning to the old activities is a more common strategy. Crocheting, cleaning house, watching television
become ways of "keeping busy," which is now the justification for living. One woman said that she missed her job when
she retired, "Until I got myself interested in keeping busy."
Another stated:

Main things I do are go to church and play bridge. Outside of
that, when I'm home, in the evenings, I watch television and
crochet. I keep busy all the time.

Again, one woman said:

> But you'd be surprised about how busy I am all the time. It seems silly, retired, and nobody but yourself. You know, you haven't got time to do things. I don't get done what I think I ought to do.

Another woman plans her day to include something that will justify the day when it comes to an end.

> If I'm active during the day, I feel better. I don't know. . . . When you feel like you've accomplished something, even if it's the washing or the ironing, you feel like you've accomplished something. But if you just sit around all day with no point in view, you don't feel as good. It's a funny thing. If you have some interest, something that holds your interest, whether it be sewing or writing letters, or doing wash or cleaning up your place, or cooking or something. But if you just lie around. . . .

By attaching new meaning to old activities, the old woman is able to justify her daily life and maintain her self-identity as not old. If she were old, she would be spending the day in a rocking chair, and, since she is active, she must not be old.

Accounts

In her relationships with her offspring, their spouses and, to a lesser degree, their children, a poor relationship is viewed by the old woman as damaging to her self-identity: stereotypical old women are forgotten by their families. Only a few informants directly expressed dissatisfaction with such a relationship, blaming the offspring, or in most cases the offspring's spouses. However, most hinted at a less than satisfactory relationship by giving accounts, excuses, or justifications for their children and in-laws not spending more time with them. Lyman and Scott (1970: 112) write:

> An account is a linguistic device employed whenever an action is subjected to valuation inquiry. . . . An account is not called for

when people engage in routine, common-sense behavior in a cultural environment that recognizes that behavior as such.

Lack of interaction with offspring, then, is not viewed as routine. Reasons must be given to explain why a son or daughter is not as attentive as the old woman would like, or others feel he or she should be, that do not tarnish her image of herself. One reason two people do not get together more often may be that one of the parties finds the time together unrewarding. This obviously is not an acceptable reason for the old woman if she is to maintain a favorable view of herself.

A common justification for lack of attention is that there is just not enough time in the day to get everything done one would like to do; other things come before Mother, and rightly so.

But as I said, if you keep a marriage together, keep a roof over their heads, keep them fed, and raise three girls, you have your hands full without worrying about your doting mother, don't you?

Or again:

I have a daughter over on 61st Street, but she works so I don't see her as often.

Even less traditional activities can be used as excuses to avoid the possible conclusion that spending time with an old woman is unrewarding. One woman recounted her daughter-in-law's weekly schedule, which included volunteer work, painting classes, a trip to the hairdressers', cleaning house, doing the laundry, and even spending the weekend with the old woman's son. This busy schedule and her son's working precluded their spending time with her, and at the same time this explanation left her self-identity intact.

She may also explain inattention by saying, in essence, "My relatives do not spend a lot of time with me because I am not an old lady yet." The fact that she is leading an independent life, that their paths rarely cross, can be a source of pride, although, perhaps a wistful pride. One old woman said in a straightforward manner:

> I've always been self-sufficient and independent and my son knows that. Without even giving it a thought, he knows that he doesn't have to worry about me.

And another pointed with pride to her relationship with her son, comparing it to some of her age peers.

> I've been more concerned about his happiness than mine. He has a nice life now. That's very important for my well being. To know that your children are all right is important. I know that there's some around here who just wait for their children to call and they're calling them forty times a day. I never have been like that because I figure they have to live. They have to hold down jobs and they can't do it if Mamma is on the phone every once in a while, crying.

This excuse makes lack of attentiveness a virtue rather than a reflection on her advanced years.

A third form refers to the "natural order of things," what Lyman and Scott (1970: 116) designate as a biological drive or "fatalistic forces" excuse, that, of course, young relatives have many interests that do not include old people. The world is seen as including some activities that are for the young only, young referring in some cases to sons and daughters only twenty years the old woman's junior. This excuse is potentially demeaning and is used not as an excuse for inattentiveness when describing nonrelatives, but as a slur. One woman described the plight of her sister-in-law.

> You know the younger people. They have their ways of doing and the older people are just left to sit and do whatever they can do.

But for sons and daughters and grandchildren to be out engaging in "young" activities is only right and "natural."

> I can't be sitting here thinking, "Oh, gee whiz, here I am alone." Sometimes my boy calls me up, but sometimes he doesn't for a week or two. And why should he? He has his life. Why should he give up his happiness with young people just because I'm his mother and bore him?

One grandmother pointed out the "naturalness" of the situation:

> They outgrow their grandmother like they do Santa Claus and other things. Used to be they'd run across the street to find you and now they'll run across the street to keep from meeting their grandma and having to explain her to their friends. You know when they are that age, they're so busy. I'm not being facetious, but they do. They outgrow their grandparents like they do Santa Claus. It's a phase of life and it isn't that they don't have any need for me now because they are busy with growing up.

If something occurs because it is "natural," because it is just the way things are, it cannot be a reflection on the old woman personally and her self-identity is left unmarred.

This "natural order of things" includes a definition of a good mother, mother-in-law, and grandmother relationship that excludes the old woman. A "good" relationship is defined by the old woman in such a way that she is an observer, or, at best, a nonvoting participant, rather than an equal partner. For example, one woman reported with pride that her daughter-in-law had said of her:

> "Oh, I've got a good mother-in-law. She never bothers. You never hear her complain." I don't know about that so much. I try not to interfere in their life. I had my life to live as I wanted to.

The old woman, then, must not make any demands on the relationship lest she give the impression that she is interfering. Another old woman reported succinctly, "We have a

very nice relationship. I try not to infringe on their privacy."
One woman explained that her son had transferred his affection from her to his wife,

> which is a good thing. That's the way it should be. So they sit and
> chit and chat and chat away more than he and I do anymore. . . .
> Anything that I want to discuss with him I can, but as far as
> personal things, well, he discusses that with his wife.

The old woman is free, and often feels obligated, to discuss
her personal affairs with her son or daughter but she does not
expect her offspring to reciprocate, and this is accepted as
"right." The old woman, then, maintains her self-identity in
an inequalitarian relationship by righteously holding to a
belief in the "natural order." That this definition of the
relationship may be accepted as natural, but not with great
conviction, is seen in bits of data such as this:

> I have a card here that I treasure from my little daughter-in-law
> that says, "To my very good friend." Now isn't that a nice thing
> to write to your mother-in-law?

When the relationship is defined as an equalitarian one, a
friendship one, even as peripherally as this, it is joyfully
noted. The old woman, then, calls on the "natural order" to
justify also the quality of the attention that does occur and,
in so doing, maintains an image of herself that is acceptable
to her.

Reciprocity

The stereotypical old woman has little to offer in relationships with other people. Valuable relationships among people
are, ideally, mutually rewarding to all parties, but old people,
by virtue of their imputed stigma and lack of resources, have
few rewards to offer others. Maintaining a belief in reciprocity, that she is giving as well as receiving, in relationships
with others, is one way to escape an image of herself as a
valueless old person.

One way to maintain this belief in reciprocity is for the old woman to feel that she is now getting a return on an investment she made in the past.

> If I ever need anything, they both will be very willing to help. When I worked I made pretty good money and I helped them a lot. I've helped them, so I think if I'm in need they would help me out, too.

This is an abstract sort of reciprocity and tends to be associated with inducing guilt feelings. It does little in the here and now to make the old woman feel deserving of affection. A here and now semblance of reciprocity can also be maintained. One woman had just spent the weekend at a lake with her son, daughter-in-law, and grandchildren, in a cabin she had purchased for them. When she purchased the cabin she explained to her son, "And I'll give it to you now. Then if I die overnight you won't have to go through court and get the $12,000." This old woman exchanged a cabin in the mountains for the right to be included in vacations.

Another old woman is quite blunt about the fact that she pays her relatives to come visit her. She may be dependent in that she needs them for transportation, household chores, outings, and company, but they get something in return. Speaking of her granddaughter's most recent visit she said:

> When she was here the other day, I, now let me see what did I do for her? I gave her groceries, filled her car up with gas, and I must have given her some money.

This old woman in almost all descriptions of visits with relatives mentions the fact that she "pays her own way and then some." She is, of course, much more blatant than most of her age peers, but, therefore, serves as an excellent example. Another less overt example is found in the following response to a question about dependency. Speaking of her daughter this woman said:

> I have to depend on her for transportation, but she depends on
> me an awful lot. I still feel useful because if anybody is sick, or
> she gets behind on her ironing or something like that, she comes
> and gets me to help her. And then I do all her sewing, too. I feel
> I'm still needed. Once school is out, they will be going to Florida
> on vacation and they will be gone for three weeks and I'm going
> over to babysit the house, do the watering, and take care of the
> mail that comes in.

By making herself useful and seeing herself as needed, she is
able to maintain this semblance of reciprocity and avoid
feeling dependent and, therefore, old. This is also done with
friends.

> I'm a doer for others and not a crier for myself and maybe that's
> why I have so many younger friends. Because I'll mind the kids.
> I'll make a dress. I'll do this and that. At the same time, I can call
> them and say, "My legs hurt me. Can you take me to the bank?"

This is an unusual case because of the age differences noted.
Reciprocity between friends of the same age is "normal" and
not particularly noteworthy. Hochschild (1973: 65-66) characterized the relationships between age peers in the public
housing project she studied as "sibling bonds."

> Most residents of Merrill Court are social siblings. The custom of
> exchanging cups of coffee, lunches, potted plants, and curtain
> checking suggest reciprocity. . . . They trade, in even measure,
> slips from house plants, kitchen utensils, and food of all sorts.
> They watched one another's apartments when someone was away
> on a visit, and they called and took calls for one another.

Reciprocity becomes an issue when self-identity is threatened
in nonegalitarian relationships.
     Failure to maintain a relationship in which exchange takes
place leads to ambivalence about the desirability of con-
tinuing the relationship.

My granddaughter comes over so much. She has a car and she's a good driver and she comes over and says, "Now, if you have any errands, let's go." Well, sometimes I feel guilty. Well, gee, she comes over here and it's tear here and tear there. She likes to do it, but I feel guilty. I feel guilty.

Carp (1972: 68) found in a study of transportation needs of the elderly that a majority of the old people in her survey sample were nervous about the skill of drivers with whom they rode, and "nearly as many disliked becoming indebted to the person who provided the ride."

One strategy, then, for maintaining self-identity in relations with others is to point out the reciprocity that is part of the relationship. In doing so the old woman avoids viewing herself as dependent, a state associated with oldness.

Discrepant Definitions of Identity

Viewed generically the situation the old widows face in finding similarities between themselves and the stereotypical old woman is one all social actors confront when they hold different definitions of themselves than are held by others with whom they interact. Much research on persons defined as deviant, either because of their appearances (social identities) or their biographies (personal identities), has focused on the difficulties of maintaining an acceptable view of self when confronted by others who hold different assumptions and definitions. Davis (1961) focuses on the visibly handicapped and how they cope to maintain a "preferred definition of self." Jackman et al. (1963) considers the problems of the professional prostitute and the way she explains her behavior in order to think of herself as a moral person. Ray (1961) focuses on the problems the reformed drug addict faces in dealing with others who adopt the attitude "once a drug addict always a drug addict." These are only a few of the many examples in the literature.

Persons who are not considered deviant find themselves in similar situations, but, because they are not considered abnormal, their strategic management of self definition has not come under close scrutiny. Most people organize their lives, or have them organized automatically by structural constraints, so that they are not with people who question their images of themselves. Professors, for example, spend most of their time with other professors or admiring (or powerless) students, rather than with members of society who question the validity of higher education and the worth of devoting a lifetime to teaching and research. Physicians spend their time with other physicians, persons in medical fields, or patients, all of whom rarely question physicians' images of themselves as competent humanitarians. When a particular group threatens their self-images, legitimate methods for eliminating those others from doctors' life space are found, such as refusal to accept Medicaid patients, ostensibly because of the burdensome paper work or low fee schedules. Women who view themselves righteously and primarily as housewives and mothers are not found in "conciousness raising" groups, and, if they are, the topics for discussion do not resemble those of groups composed of self-proclaimed feminists. Classical music buffs rarely find themselves in situations in which they must defend their taste in music (Benson, 1971), but, if they do, may credibly explain their position, for it is shared by others. For "normals," then, the social world is organized in such a way that self-identity is rarely questioned and, if it is, active or passive withdrawal from those situations is relatively easy and seen as legitimite.

This is not to say that professors, physicians, mothers, and feminists, do not have doubts about their respective self-identities. A physician, for example, must occasionally ask him or herself, "What if I really am motivated by economic self-interest?" Feminists must wonder if they really are simply "man haters." A favorable view of self, even under ideal circumstances, may be more difficult to maintain than is often assumed. "Defense mechanisms," which are usually relegated to the status of neurotic or psychotic symptoms, can more accurately be considered as positive, necessary, and ingenious methods for protecting self from the paralyzing effects of doubt (Lofland, 1976).

The old widows whose social worlds are under analysis here are more like the "deviants" than the "normals" in that their worlds are not neatly compartmentalized. Associating primarily with others who see them as they see themselves is difficult. The stereotypes about oldness are pervasive. Indeed, the old women share them. There are fewer others available to validate their self-images than there are for "normals."

All of the examples above are of actors who view themselves as better (more competent, wiser, more intelligent) than others with whom they may come into contact. Some actors may be pleasantly surprised to find that others are willing to accept them as they think of themselves. Research on attitudes toward the old shows that the old are not consistently viewed negatively (Brubaker and Powers, 1976), and the analysis here emphasizes the ambiguous nature of applying the label "old." There is, then, a very real possibility that those with whom the old widows interact have a higher opinion of them than is expected. The strategies the old women and others use to protect their self-images may prevent them from discovering that they are, in fact, admired by others, or at least, that others are willing to relegate their oldness or other attributes to the status of a basic identity. Evidence to support this is found in Kitsuse's (1962) analysis of attitudes of informants toward acquaintances whom they discovered were homosexuals. He found that the informants' opinions changed only slightly. By encapsulating themselves, the old widows, and others with weak stigmas, may be preventing themselves from discovering that situations are much less negative than they assume.

Summary

It is certainly not news that members of stigmatized groups find ways to protect their images of themselves and old women are not exceptions. In encounters with others and encounters with self they are able to put forth points of view and explanations and to manage daily rounds so that their behavior and relationships are not seen as "typical" of old women generally, and, thus, are able to maintain acceptable self-images. Old women occupy a peculiar position because they have fewer ways than most "normal" members of society in which to redeem themselves and many of the strategies they use to maintain an acceptable self-identity separate them still further from the mainstream of social life.

Chapter 5

THE IMPORTANCE OF SETTING IN THE
LIVES OF OLD WIDOWS[1]

Little attention has been given to the subjective meaning attached to settings in which persons lead their social lives and the familiar people in those settings who are not role partners. Rather, the focus has been on the development and maintenance of "community" within particular settings (cf. Hochschild, 1973; Johnson, 1971; Ross, 1977; Suttles, 1968). "Community" does develop within settings. Indeed, "spacially circumscribed area" (Karp et al., 1977: 65) or "territory" is part of the definition of community, as are "we-feeling" and "social organization" (Ross, 1977: 5). However, in looking for signs and outcomes of "community" within particular settings, the perspective of persons residing within those communities is often lost. To focus only on community aspects of settings is to lose an important insight into the ways in which people's self-identities are affected by their subjective feelings about their places in the settings in which they lead their daily lives.

This chapter addresses the relationship between meaning attached to settings by individual social actors and their self-identities. The reflection of self is mirrored in persons with whom individuals interact (Cooley, 1967), but it is also mirrored in settings which are comprised of physical objects and persons who are only faces to which individuals have attached meaning. This dimension of the looking-glass self is often either ignored or glossed over as unimportant. This is not surprising: the settings in which people lead their daily lives are taken-for-granted. What it is about these familiar settings that gives meaning to people's lives is difficult to articulate even for the most observant social actor. In addition, situations in which settings can be divorced from the social interaction that takes place within them are difficult to find. In looking closely at the social worlds of old widows I was confronted with the existence of this situation for some of the informants, "newcomers" who had moved to the settings in which I found them after they were old.

In the analysis that follows, comparisons are made between informants who saw themselves as "residents" and informants who saw themselves as "newcomers" as those self-designations relate to the informants' social and self-identities. After clarifying these ideal types, contributors to this self-designation are examined, that is, the nonhuman or physical aspects of their settings and the people who shared those settings with them. Finally, strategies for maintaining "resident" status are shown to be more limited for the old than they are for younger members of society. Throughout the chapter, attention is paid to what other analysts of social life have said about the relationship between settings and self-identity.

Newcomers and Residents

Both the way an old woman perceives herself and the way others view her in a particular setting are dependent to some degree on her status as "resident" or "newcomer." These were the common-sense categories used by the informants: there were "new" old people, those who had moved to the setting relatively recently, and "old" old people, those who had spent a major portion of their lives in the setting.

The social identity of an old woman rests in part on her status as newcomer or resident. A long-time resident may assume that she has a known biography. The woman who has grown old in a particular setting is more likely to be seen by others in that setting as wrinkled and gray-headed, but as essentially the same person she has always been. In Travisano's (1970: 604) words, her age is more likely to be a basic rather than a general identity; that is, "to be woven throughout" interaction with others rather than "central to interaction." She may be, "John the successful lawyer's mother;" or "the woman who has always been active in politics;" or "the woman whose husband left her and for good reason;" but regardless of the positive or negative evaluation of her character and biography, it is known, and potentially knowable to others. She has a reputation. Of course, all participants in the setting may not be aware of her reputation, but those with whom the old woman is most likely to come into contact will be, and recent recruits who voice the assumption that there is a causal relationship between advanced age and behavior, as I did on several occasions, will be corrected by long-time residents.

The resident has a reputation; the newcomer is not so lucky.[2] She arrives on the scene already old. Her move to the setting was probably precipitated by a negatively evaluated status passage. Recent retirement, either for herself or her husband, widowhood, or decreased physical capacity are the most likely explanations of a move to be closer to a son, a daughter, or other relative. Even decisions to move to retirement communities may be based on proximity of kin rather than weather (Barker, 1966). The most salient characteristic of newcomers, then, is their oldness and their imputed, and often accepted, devalued status as no longer independent, financially, emotionally, or physically. Other status attributes may offset the devalued ones. Presence of a husband, physical health and stamina, an automobile, a well-known relative already living in the setting,[3] are examples of characteristics that afford an old woman higher status. All things being equal, however, the resident will have the advantage over the newcomer.

The salience of oldness for newcomers is evident in the monikers attached to them. One newcomer is called "grandma" at the church she attends.

> One of the men at the church said the other day, "Do you mind their calling you 'grandma'?" There are people there over 65 years of age calling me "grandma" because they heard my grandkids calling me "grandma" over there. I said, "No, I don't mind at all," and he said, "Well, I don't want them calling me 'grandpa'."

And if he is a resident he is probably safe. Other church members have aged with him and know him as a total person rather than only as an old person.

An old woman who is a resident is more likely to have her behavior accepted or normalized because it is seen as part of her character rather than caused by her age. This statement is simplistic. Character and oldness are, of course, not independent explanations of behavior. However, residents can expect "character" to play a greater part in others' assessment of their behavior than newcomers can. A resident can say, "I'm an outspoken old woman. I'm a character around town, I'm sure." This same woman, when she is "mad as a wet hen about something" can swear at the mayor over the phone with impunity because it is expected of her. She is acting "in character."

A newcomer does not have the same right. Moving to the new setting may be viewed by others and by herself as an admission that she is too old to cope, either with an environment or without support from a relative. She must try to

create a favorable social identity with two strikes against her
from the start. One informant reacted to others' ignorance of
her biography: "As I told someone one time, 'Don't think
I've always been fat and gray-headed and sat here on Clover
Lane. I haven't been here all my life'." Others react with less
fighting spirit when they find that there is no place for them
in the social web of a new setting.

> There are days and days I don't talk to anybody. See, I can't
> make friends because they don't know me and when I try to get
> to know someone, they have their own friends, their own chil-
> dren, their own in-laws. They have their brothers and sisters, and
> you're nobody really. They're nice to you but they don't, it
> seems, want to take another in.

This degree of felt isolation is extreme, but exemplifies
feelings that other newcomers express more obliquely.

For the purpose of this analysis, newcomer and resident
must be defined by the informants themselves rather than by
objective criteria. In subjective terms, resident refers to the
feeling by the old person that she is known as a person rather
than as an old person, that she feels "at home" in the world
around her. Lack of this feeling is alluded to often by
newcomers: for residents it is not even an issue. One newcomer expressed this in terms of a dichotomy between physical presence and emotional presence: "I live in Sunnyville but
my house and heart are in Camptown. My son lives in
Sunnyville and he's a pretty good crutch to lean on."
Another old woman is adamant about the imprudence of old
women leaving familiar surroundings to move to be near
relatives. Referring to a neighbor she said:

> She did things wrong. She sold out where she was and came out
> here where she didn't know anybody and when you get older,
> that's kind of bad. You don't make friends as easy. She wishes
> now she'd kept her place. She has a daughter here, but all her old
> friends are back there. She should have stayed there. That's why I

don't want my sister to sell her home. Keep it. Stay there. Those apple trees—she and Harry planted them, and she watched them grow up and mature.

Resident and newcomer are ideal types and thereby make the distinction appear simpler than it is in fact. For example, how one makes the transition from newcomer to resident is not altogether clear. Willingness and ability to be assertive, socially or politically, may enable a "newcomer" to become a "resident" fairly quickly, while acquiescence in the newcomer status may perpetuate the status indefinitely. In addition, the availability of a niche in an ongoing setting may facilitate a newcomer's becoming a resident. For example, one informant's status had changed fairly quickly from newcomer to resident in the trailer park in which she lived. Her widowed son was the handyman and she delivered the morning and evening newspapers in the park. This case also illustrates another dimension of this typification. Outside the park her status changed to newcomer in that she felt somewhat out of place. The size of the territory in which residents are able to retain their feeling of belonging, then, also varies, but having one geographical setting in which one feels like a resident, be it a trailor park or a city, may be as important as having one confidant (Lowenthal and Haven, 1968).

Features of the Setting

Contributing to a sense of being a resident are familiarity with physical aspects of the setting and familiarity with people who share the setting. Residents are much more likely to be familiar with both the physical aspects of the setting and the people in the setting than are newcomers, although rapid changes in the settings themselves, as in transitional urban areas, can destroy this sense of belonging even for those who, from an objective standpoint, would be considered residents.

Physical Aspects

Lack of familiarity with physical surroundings is problematic to newcomers, but not merely because of the inconvenience of having to learn the map of a new locale. Knowledge of a physical setting provides assurance that the world can be taken-for-granted. The following informant's reference to home is a town in another state which she left three years prior to the interview to move to a town in which her daughter resides.

> I don't care too much about going out alone in a strange place. There's too much going on. Now that's in a strange place. Now if I were at home, I wouldn't think anything about it. But when you're in a strange neighborhood and everyone you meet is a stranger, it makes quite a difference to you.

An unfamiliar setting increases her sense of vulnerability to strangers. Another newcomer who has lived in a town over ten years limits the number of miles she drives because she is overpowered by the unknown physical world.

> I don't want to lose my license. So I go and get my groceries and I go to church. Once in a while, I'll drive up to the next town. If I know exactly where I'm going, don't have to look for any of the streets, I can do pretty well.

Yet another newcomer who has lived in the community ten years and drives an automobile comments, "But I just don't volunteer to go around and pick up people. I don't know the town too well."[4] She has acquiesced in her newcomer status and finds navigating in an unfamiliar setting too large an obstacle to surmount.

The settings from which the old women moved, leaving behind their status of residents to become newcomers, had a familiarity that could be taken-for-granted. In Polanyi's (1967) words, there was a "tacit dimension"[5] to the towns in which they resided, a world taken-for-granted in which they could do their daily lives. The setting provided order without their conscious awareness. Illustrative of this "tacit dimension" is Schutz's (1964: 108) discussion of the seemingly trivial things missed by soldiers away from home.

> All these things, badly missed if not available were probably not particularly appreciated so long as they were accessible at any time. They had just their humble place among the collective value "homely things." Thus, home means one thing to the man who never has left it, another thing to the man who dwells far from it, and still another to him who returns.

Residents do refer to the way the town used to be: "Mildred was born right where Ruth sits at the desk all day at the bank;" "There used to be a hog farm where that new apartment building is." However, residents were present when the changes occurred and were able to incorporate them into their worlds of the familiar.

This tacit dimension, then, is only clear to newcomers for whom it is made painfully obvious by its sudden, and, at least for some, irreplaceable loss. Fried found a similar response in urban slum dwellers who were forced to relocate by urban renewal.

> It is a sense of belonging someplace in a particular place which is quite familiar and easily delineated, in a wide area in which one feels "at home." This is the core of meaning of the local area. And this applies for many people who have few close relationships within the area. Even familiar and expectable streets and houses, faces at the windows and people walking by, personal greetings and impersonal sounds may serve to designate the concrete foci of a sense of belonging somewhere and may provide special kinds of interpersonal and social meaning to a region one defines as "home" [Fried, 1963: 154].

Their reactions to loss of their neighborhood, Fried characterized as grief, and the above description of the importance to his sample of a familiar physical setting was also apparent among the informants of this research.

More dramatic examples of the importance of the physical features of the setting to a subjective sense of belonging are found in the reactions of survivors of natural and man-made disasters. Lifton (1969: 30), in analyzing the reactions of survivors of the bomb dropped in Hiroshima, stresses that in the first days following the explosion, those alive faced,

> annihilation of self and of individual identity, along with the sense of having virtually experienced that annihilation; and destruction of the non-human environment, of *the field or context of ones existence,* and therefore of one's overall sense of "being-in-the-world" [emphasis altered].

Talking to the residents over one year after the occurrence, Erikson (1976: 62) describes the effects on the survivors of the collapse of a dam, causing a major flood which destroyed homes and property along Buffalo Creek, West Virginia.

> Most of the survivors never realized the extent to which they relied on the rest of the community to reflect back a sense of meaning to them, never understood the extent to which they depended on others to supply them with a point of reference. When survivors say they feel "adrift," "displaced," "uprooted," "lost," they mean that they do not seem to belong to anything and that there are no longer any familiar social landmarks to help them fix their position in time and space. They are depressed, yes, but it is a depression born of the feeling that they are suspended pointlessly in the middle of nowhere.

Familiar Faces

Familiarity with physical settings cannot be divorced from the people who populate that setting (Lofland, 1973). Both supply a feeling of continuity for the old woman. In most discussions by social gerontologists of old women's relationships with others, those others are confined to spouse, offspring, siblings, and, occasionally, friends and neighbors. Others whose relationship to the old woman is less easily defined are also important, as Fried observed, in that they provided the taken-for-granted background for the definition of self. As the newcomer cited above indicated, a strange neighborhood also means strange people. The chance that someone met casually on the street might be a known other appears to supply a comfortable background in which to act, while, more importantly, the absence of that knowledge makes navigating the neighborhood problematic.

The setting has different characteristics for old women who are residents and old women who are newcomers. The resident may assume that her biography is public knowledge. Informally addressing a small gathering of old women, a long-time resident prefaced a somewhat personally revealing story about herself with, "You all know me." Whether the old woman was in fact known by those she was addressing is irrelevant. Rather the important point is that the speaker assumed that she, as a long-time citizen of her town, was known to those present, and acted on that assumption. This assumption is not available to the newcomer.

For the resident, merely reading the local newspaper, including, of course, the obituaries, means covering familiar territory and names of people who may not be personally known to her but who have some likelihood of being familiar, even if indirectly. One resident mentioned a fellow club member who had died the day before. "She has two marvelous sons. You build up a very close feeling with these people you've lived with for fifty years." In this instance, the subjective nature of resident status is clear. The woman describes as "close" her feelings about two men whom she rarely sees, but knowledge of them and of their affairs increases the feeling of continuity in her life.

Newcomers live in settings in which they are strangers and feel like strangers. Other participants in the setting are primarily recent acquaintances, except for extended family members for whom the old women are occupants of well-defined roles. One newcomer stated, "Of course, everyone is a stranger to me here and not going to church I don't meet anyone." Another woman, objectively a resident, in fact, a newcomer, is afraid to go out alone.

> In Middletown I don't know anybody. I used to know everybody who lived here years and years ago. Now I don't know anybody and they don't know me.

Likewise, a change in the population of the area may serve to destroy a sense of belonging. New neighbors, whether from a move of only a few blocks or from neighborhood transition as in some urban areas, can destroy a sense of being a resident.

Limited Strategies

In order to gain resident status, an old woman may simply remain in a setting. However, if she is not lucky enough to live in a small, relatively stable one, she has only to remain in her house or apartment through the years and she may change from resident to newcomer through no act of her own; neighbors may move away and buildings may be removed. Residents were in the minority among the informants for this research. The adjectives *small* and *stable* do not characterize the settings in which most persons live in the United States.

Newcomers often spoke wistfully of homes they had left behind. Many wished that they might permanently return to the places they had left, but felt it was impossible. When they met someone from their hometown or states, they were clearly excited. One woman who met an old friend at the pharmacy and talked with her for "a long time" remembered the day with wonder: "I was happy all day."

Once the move is made, however, the status of resident may be impossible to reclaim. One informant had moved to

be near her children when her husband retired because he was
in poor health.

> It was a bad move. I don't like it here. I lost him in 1964. I guess
> I'm stuck to stay because I don't have folks anymore up there.
> Oh, I have a lot of in-laws, nieces and nephews, but I don't count
> them in.

Another informant actually attempted to go "home," but
found that she was no longer a resident of the community in
which she had lived for so many years. She returned defeated
to the town in which she resided with her daughter. Too
often the enormity of the sacrifice involved in moving to be
nearer her offspring is not realized by the old mother until it
is too late. By then, her fellow residents in the setting have
followed her example, or she has followed theirs, and there is
no longer a community of people to which to return. Resi-
dential settings may appear to be stable entities, but, in fact,
they change from day to day in ways that residents take for
granted.[6]

Taking up residence in age-homogeneous housing is one
way to cope with this dilemma. At least theoretically, no one
who lives in a retirement community or a "senior citizens"
housing project is a resident. All are newcomers, and all were,
at least minimally, old when they arrived on the scene. In
these communities, old age as a social attribute on which to
differentiate among people is eliminated, allowing other attributes of the residents to come to the fore and a microworld
revolving around these new definitions to develop (Hochschild, 1973; Rosow, 1974; Ross, 1977). In addition, inhabi-
tants are protected from demeaning imputations from younger
others. This is more generally, of course, one of the factors
affecting the rise of any ghetto. Many of the informants who
had applied for public housing and been rejected because
their incomes clearly made them ineligible, were still anxious
to move into public housing because of the occupants rather

than the low rent. Others had turned down age-integrated
public housing, preferring to continue paying more for rent
while waiting for an opening in a senior citizens complex.

Summary

The focus of the analysis in this chapter has been on the
settings in which old widows do their daily lives. Analysis of
the data revealed an important subjective distinction among
the informants. Some informants were "residents" in that
they had lived in settings most of their lives and felt comfortable in them while others were "newcomers" who lacked this
feeling of being at home in their settings. Residents viewed
themselves and assumed that they were viewed by others as
people grown old while newcomers assumed that they were
viewed simply as old people.

The subjective feeling of belonging in a setting was ap-
proached from two vantage points, the physical aspects of
setting and those who shared the setting with the informant.
The physical aspects of settings in which persons do their
daily lives have a "tacit dimension"; there is a great deal
about the settings in which people act that is known about
and taken-for-granted, but is only recognized consciously
when it is removed. Even then, what is missing is difficult to
articulate. Familiar settings, then, are valuable assets that are
often ignored by people making decisions to move. For the
old, familiar settings are especially valuable because of their
likely devalued status in new settings where their oldness
becomes a general identity. People in settings who are only
acquaintances or familiar faces rather than role partners were
also shown to be important contributors to the feeling of
being a resident.

In attempting to maintain a sense of familiarity with the
settings in which they lead their daily lives the old widows
must often play a passive role. They cannot control social
change or the deaths, geographical mobility, or physical

impairments, of friends. One active strategy is to move into retirement communities to share with others in making a community in which everyone is a newcomer, making resident an easier status to achieve. Controversy rages over the advisability of utilizing this strategy.

Most of the time social actors may take for granted who they are, and settings confirm the taken-for-granted assumptions. However, both social change and changes in individuals' lives may make previously assigned meanings problematic and reassessment necessary. The old widows are not alone in facing situations in which they must reassess who they are. This is a society characterized by geographical mobility and a status change from resident to newcomer is not an unusual occurrence. For younger people being in a new setting may be stressful (Booth and Camp, 1974), but the move to a new setting is usually perceived as lineal (Lee, 1950). That is, the move to the new setting does not make identity and biography problematic but is seen as a logical, next step in confirmation of a positively evaluated identity. The effects of such moves are probably not as negative as is true of old widows. As a case in point, Zimmer (1970: 83) writes:

> On the basis of a case study of a single community, it seems that migration does limit participation in community activities, but the initial limiting influences of migration are only temporary for these types of behavior, at least in that, with time, migrants either equal or exceed the natives in level of participation. When migrants first enter the new community they are much less active in the formal structure than are the natives, but with time their participant rate increases. The adjustment takes at least 5 years, however, and in some types of behavior migrants possessing low status characteristics never do attain the same level of participation as the natives. The possession of high status personal characteristics facilitates the adjustment.

The old widows who are newcomers qualify as possessors of "low status characteristics" and analysis of newcomer status from their perspective lays bare the forces operating. By ignoring the importance of the setting in which persons are old and extolling the virtues of the viable extended family, social gerontologists have ignored an important component in the maintenance of an acceptable self-identity for old women.

NOTES

1. This chapter appeared in slightly revised form in *Qualitative Sociology,* 1979, 1(3):35-52.

2. Having a known past is not always an asset, for a person with a known past must act "in character," according to others' expectations, making personal change difficult. But changing friends to change identity probably becomes increasingly difficult, and, more important here, less desired as aging occurs. The social statuses accompanying old age are not valued ones and positively evaluated attributes are more likely to be dependent on what one has done, rather than what one is doing or will do. Old people who are happy to leave a town because "everyone knew everyone else," as one informant was, are probably unusual. Even a "lowly" past that is known is better than having *old* become one's most salient characteristic.

3. Old women usually move to be near a daughter rather than a son (Lopata, 1973; Hochschild, 1973). One old woman who is a newcomer moved to live near a son. In his prestigious occupational role he receives much attention in the local newspapers. Her status is greatly elevated by his. This newcomer would not be in this position if her offspring were female and married, a more typical situation. Unless the newcomer bragged openly about the relationship, acquaintances and strangers would not know that she and her daughter were related. Most old women are not lucky enough to have famous sons in the same community.

4. This newcomer has also given up driving at night, as many older drivers have, regardless of their status as newcomers or residents. However, this is explained as not seeing well at night rather than as not knowing the town, an important difference.

5. Polanyi (1967: 4) writes, "I shall reconsider human knowledge from the fact that we can know more than we can tell. This fact seems obvious enough; but it is not easy to say exactly what it means. We know a person's face, and can recognize it among a thousand, indeed among a million. Yet we usually cannot tell how we recognize a face we know. So most of this knowledge cannot be put into words."

6. Schutz (1964: 113) provides insight:

The change in the system of relevance and in the degree of intimacy . . . is differently experienced by the absent one and by the home group. The latter continues its daily life within the customary pattern. Certainly, this pattern, too, will have changed and even in a more or less abrupt way. But those at home, although aware of this change, lived together through the changing world, experienced it as changing in immediacy, adapted their interpretive system, and adjusted themselves entirely, but it changed as a system; it was never disrupted and broken down; even in its modification it is still an appropriate device for mastering life.

Chapter 6

BEING AN OLD MOTHER IN THE
UNEXTENDED EXTENDED FAMILY

Much research has focused on the extended family for two not entirely disparate reasons. On the theoretical side, research has been in response to the assumed dichotomy in family forms represented by preindustrial or agrarian societies and by industrial societies. In the former, kinship groups are prevalent and important; in the latter, the extended family gives way to the isolated nuclear family consisting of parents and nonadult offspring, leaving the old parents to fend for themselves, or so the theory holds. Beginning in the 1950s the validity of the assumption came under empirical examination, a continuum rather than a dichotomy was found to represent reality more accurately, and the "modified extended family" (Litwak, 1960) was declared the "Unheralded Structure in Current Conceptualizations of Family Functioning" (Sussman and Burchinal, 1962). Research since that time has delineated the nature of the relationship between parents and their adult offspring under a variety of circumstances (Sussman, 1965).

Litwak (1960: 10) defines the "modified extended family" as consisting of "a series of nuclear families bound together on an equalitarian basis, with a strong emphasis on the extended family bonds as an end value." Old widowed mothers, however, do not qualify as nuclear families, making their position in this theoretical structure somewhat ambiguous.[1] Comparison of adult-offspring-widowed-mother relationships with adult-offspring-still-married-mother relationships indicates that they differ: obligation rather than enjoyment is more likely to characterize the relationships when the mother is widowed, especially for sons (Adams, 1968). If old widowed mothers are to be included in this "unheralded structure," an examination of their position in this structure is in order.

The related reason for studying the extended family has been to formulate informed social policy for the aged. This research goes hand in hand with the theoretical studies for reasons that can, in part, be traced to sources of funding, and demonstrates that old parents are not isolated from family members. Isolation is most often determined by number of visits among family members and number and types of services performed (Shanas, 1962; Shanas et al., 1968). These studies also maintain that social security and other pension programs are not undermining feelings of filial responsibility (Schorr, 1960; Townsend, 1957). For both of these purposes, merely demonstrating the existence of an extended family structure is adequate.

By these researchers' own admission, however, their studies are methodologically inappropriate to analyze the quality of the relationships that have been found to exist. Stenhouwer recognizes that he cannot generalize beyond the limitations of his data and acknowledges that his data do not enable us to evaluate the attitudes that lie behind the pattern of contacts as we observe it. Nor does it evaluate the quality of family relationships, or the relative importance of family contacts in relation to the total network of contacts that may be maintained by older persons [Shanas et al., 1968: 181].

Rosow (1967: 201-202) also points out the limits to understanding the quality of old parent-offspring relationships of data obtained through questionnaires.

Further, our information is largely structured; we have no systematic qualitative data on the nuances of interaction by which to analyze the subtler aspects of the relationship. We can only deal with the general dimensions of the problem.

The data for this analysis, then, were gathered with the intent of discovering the "subtler aspects of these relationships."

The argument to be developed in this chapter is that, although the old mother's relations with her children are very important to her, the current structure of the "modified extended family" does not give the old mother a viable position in this group. An exchange perspective is used to elucidate the relationship between the old mothers and their offspring. The old mother is shown to be in a subordinate position in her family because she is very likely to have only her offspring as a source of "moral support" and needed services and at the same time very little to offer in return. In using the exchange theory perspective, I am not suggesting that it is a perspective that explains all behavior, but, rather that as a heuristic device, it makes clear the superordinate/ subordinate relationship with which old mothers must deal.

Importance of Offspring

The informants for this research support the findings in previous research (Rosow, 1967)—that the old widow's offspring are of paramount importance to her. They provide "moral support" that is not available or, perhaps more accurately, not considered dependable from nonrelatives. For example, one old woman rejected my assertion that I was her friend, first, on the basis of our ages being too discrepant, and second, and of more importance here, on the basis that she could not depend on me because we were unrelated. This belief is alluded to often by the informants and it is important to consider to what extent the self-fulfilling prophecy is at work here.

The primary importance of relatives, and especially offspring, is evident in the following data. One widow stated that she sees her family often.

> That's why I stay in this area. I wouldn't know what to do if I didn't have them. I feel sorry for a couple that didn't have children. . . . It seems that they don't have anyone. . . . But having children, they tell me, my grandchildren, "Don't worry, Grandma. We'll take care of you." And I know they will.

Children, then, provide moral support that is not considered to be available from other sources. Another widow stated, "I have a wonderful family. I never feel alone. I think that's something, when you have somebody who loves you." Many old widows would agree with one of their age peers who stated bluntly, "My son is the main thing in my life now." Even those who are not accustomed to seeing their offspring often, place great importance on the relationship. Frequent interaction, however, is desirable.

> I usually see them [offspring] once a week, but this week I didn't, and when I don't see them once a week, I feel lost. If it's only just for a few minutes. I guess everybody feels the same way. Your family is your family. Nobody can take the place of your family. You can fight with them like the dickens, but you don't stay mad.

What are the ramifications of the assumption that the family is all important? The answer to this question will become clear following, first, a discussion of the position of the old widow in the family group, and second, an analysis of her position from an exchange perspective.

How Extended is the Family?

What is the old widow's position in the family? This is, of course, a complex question, the answer to which depends on some important sociological variables, such as social class, and some intrafamilial variables such as number, sex, and ages of offspring and grandchildren, and geographical proximity of family members (Shanas et al., 1968: 227-257). The widows who were informants for the research reported here represent a wide combination of these variables, yet their descriptions of relationships with offspring and grandchildren are remarkably similar. If only typical survey questions[2] were used as a source of information, many of the informants would appear to have a well-integrated role in their families. However, descriptions of their relationships are much like the descriptions of those who would appear much more isolated in a survey. The similarities in these two types is found in the larger societal and, therefore, personal expectations of the role of the old mother and mother-in-law in the extended family.

When a mother's daughter or son becomes an adult either by marrying or becoming economically self-sufficient, her relationship with that offspring changes. Brabec (1975: 7) describes her reaction to the change in her status:

The loss of an "everyday place" has led to loss of *significant* place in the lives of my adult sons. Although our geographical separation is measured by only eight city blocks, the cultural separation—mothers and sons—is measured in light years. This is the irreconcilable loss of my middle years and the one that seems the most unnatural. It is not enough to have other interests, strong concerns, other people; I continue to need this primary relationship as an integral, rather than a peripheral, part of my life. I believe the need is mutual, although not mutually felt. We are

[not] "supposed to" need each other anymore. They are not "supposed to" learn from my experiences, my mistakes and now my feminism, even though they inherit many of my characteristics—my problems too—and, above all, the same culture and its problems. Is it logical for this most primary relationship to become so peripheral? Isn't being largely separated from those to whom you were once closest, those you still care most about, not only illogical but irrational and inhuman? Could it be that nature never intended the human nest to be so empty?

There is some evidence that lower-class mothers may not lose so quickly their "significant place" (Komarovsky, 1962; Townsend, 1957). However, in Komarovsky's (1962) study of blue-collar couples, the oldest respondents were under forty years of age with the bulk of the respondents being in their twenties. Few of their parents were over sixty years of age. The assumption cannot be made that adult children in their twenties will continue to have the same relationships with their parents and in-laws when they are in their fifties and sixties and their parents and in-laws are in their seventies and eighties. The ages of Komarovsky's respondents is not unusual: in much of the research on parent-adult offspring relationships, the parents are "middle-aged" (Sussman, 1965). As mothers age, however, it appears that the differences between social classes begin to converge (Shanas et al., 1968: 227-257) and the old mothers' positions in their families become similar. Shanas is focusing, as are most researchers, on differences among old people who are members of different social classes (white collar, blue collar, service workers, and agricultural workers). Her comparisons emphasize differences. These differences are statistically significant, but they are relatively small in most cases. As she indicates, social class may not be as important a variable as number and gender of children. For example, the mother-daughter bond appears to be the most salient intergenerational relationship (Townsend, 1957; Young and Geertz, 1961), and the presence of a daughter or two may have more predictive value for integration of the old widow into the family than social class.

When sons and daughters marry, their loyalties are expected to shift. In a sense, the mother becomes a mother-in-law to her offspring as well, for she is expected to take second place to her new in-law's demands and expectations of her offspring. The definition of the mother's relationship with her offspring and in-laws is ambiguous, and continues to be so as she grows older. Duvall, in a now-classic description of in-law relationships, points to the dilemma in which the mother-in-law finds herself.

> Many a mother-in-law sounds baffled, bewildered, and bitter in her role. She reports that anything she does is misconstrued by her sons- and daughters-in-law. If she leaves them alone, she is being neglectful; if she is nice to them, she is being two-faced; if she appears interested in what they are doing, she is meddling; if she keeps out of their affairs, she is not interested in them—she just can't win [Duvall, 1954: 172]!

The mother-in-law, then, depends on her offspring and his or her spouse for a definition of the relationship to become established. The definition will, of course, change with time and circumstances, and is negotiable, but the younger generation appears to have the deciding vote, as Mrs. M. from Rhode Island points out.

> My method in trying to be a good mother-in-law has been to mind my own business, do anything I could to make the children happy and expect nothing. It has worked to the extent that I think they are happy. I am still minding my own business and my expectations have been fulfilled and I have nothing! Except in a few rare cases, I am quite sure *the mother-in-law is only what the young people make her* [Duvall, 1954: 174, emphasis added].

Herein lies the key to the position of the old widow in the family, and, as will become apparent below, the seeds of an unbalanced relationship. She must abide by the definition of her role as set down by her now adult offspring, or risk being labeled an interfering mother-in-law. Deutscher (1962) sees the myth of the interfering mother-in-law as a "conditioning device." Women do not wish to view themselves or be viewed by others as "typical" interfering mothers-in-law, and, therefore, accept uncritically their children's behavior, regardless of their own beliefs about its wisdom.

"Noninterference" is difficult to actualize for it depends on the expectations of the role partner rather than personal judgment. What will be interpreted as interference? Brabec (1976: 9) quotes from an anonymous letter written to her:

> If we dare ask our adult children, "When will we see each other again?" it's not taken as an expression of interest and affection, but as a manipulative ploy, an "unreasonable demand" from which they must defend themselves, and in doing so, of course, they must not feel guilty.

Old mothers, then, are left to watch, at times in horror:

> We baby-sit, help with the finances and all that rubbish, but we must never interfere, never touch. It is as if we were doing enough, just by being. I know grandparents who sit in horror, but in a silence that is superhuman, at some of the things they see the young up to today [Pauley, 1973].

Even their inclusion in family gatherings, which on the surface appears to be active participation, is often merely ritual. For example, old mothers are included in family get togethers, but are not in on the planning stage.

> We get together and have feeds. Everybody brings a dish. There's about sixteen when they all get together. They'll probably plan something for the Fourth. I haven't heard them say anything about it yet.

Simply including old mothers in the event is considered enough. Old women are merely expected to "be" rather than participate, as in the case of one old woman whose daughter-in-law (the wife of a deceased son) invited her for a visit in Hawaii, all expenses paid. Once there, however, the old woman stayed in the apartment while her daughter-in-law worked during the day. At night her host was too tired to go out. Her two-week vacation in Hawaii included only one outing that coincided with a half-day business trip (which, incidentally, left the old woman with little to relate about her trip to Hawaii but a description of airplane travel). Another old woman spoke of her last-minute inclusion in a weekend trip that she was invited to join simply because of a well-timed phone call.

> My daughter-in-law called up. No, I think I had called her up about something. My son answered and he wanted to know how I was and I told him. Then, I talked to my daughter-in-law and she said my son was out waiting in the car and that they were going down to the Bay. It wasn't more than ten minutes after that she called back and said, "Do you think you're too sick to take a ride down?" So I said, "It was yesterday that I had the headache" (but it always takes me the full day and the next day to get over it). "No," I said, "I think maybe the fresh air would do me good." So she said, "We'll pick you up." So they came up and got me and we went down to the Bay. It was a nice outing.

Old mothers who attempt to be active participants may be rebuffed.

> I had a run in with my granddaughter when I lived with my daughter while I was looking for a place. I loved doing her housework and taking care of the children, but I would forget that they were my grandchildren instead of my children, and I would correct them. They resented being corrected by me.

When an old mother finds someone who is unfamiliar with the ritual enactment of a family gathering, she may be pleasantly surprised, as was one informant who was taken with her granddaughter's new boyfriend because she could talk with him: "I like to talk to them, but they've always been bashful talking to Grandma."

A brief summary of the developing argument is that being an old, widowed mother in a "family" context is problematic. The old mother's relationship with her offspring may be viewed as the most important relationship in her life at the same time that her place in her childrens' lives has become ritualized. An exchange perspective is useful for articulating this dilemma.

Distribution of Power

Dowd (1975) has made a convincing theoretical argument for viewing the process of aging under the umbrella of exchange theory. He points out that the two competing "theories" in social gerontology, disengagement theory, which theorizes that aged persons who withdraw from social life are better adjusted (Cumming and Henry, 1961), and activity theory, which theorizes that aged people actively involved in social life are better adjusted, that is, have higher morale and life satisfaction (Lemon et al., 1972), take for granted the inevitability of fewer social contacts for the aged and that neither

> attempts to offer anything but the most perfunctory of explanations for the *decreased social interaction* itself. Rather, this phenomenon is given the status of a sociological "given"; that is, it is treated as something requiring no additional explanation [Dowd, 1975: 585].

Dowd argues that exchange theory, which focuses on the rewards and costs of interaction to persons who have differential access to power, can better explain decreasing social interaction as well as allow for the wide variety of responses people make to the aging process.

Homans (1958) points out that everyday social interaction between people is often viewed in economic terms by participants. They evaluate the costs and rewards of particular interactions with each other and arrive at a rate of social exchange which maximizes the rewards and minimizes the costs to each. People, of course, have different types and amounts of rewards to offer one another depending in part on the various statuses they occupy in the social world. Age is an important variable for distributing valuable statuses, that is, positions which include access to rewards, especially at the ends of the age continuum (van den Berghe, 1973). For example, in American society, the aged are forced to abdicate their positions in the labor force simply because they have accumulated seventy years which Dowd (1975) sees as the institutionalization of an exchange by the aged of their places in the labor force for increased leisure time supported by other members of society.[3]

Much of the discussion of the determinants of status of the aged in societies (Rosow, 1974: 3-7; Cowgill and Holmes, 1972; Cowgill, 1974) fits into an exchange perspective by pointing to likely power resources or, in this case, lack of them. However, explicate use of the exchange model has the advantage of conceptualizing the relationship of the aged and others in society as process rather than as statically determined. The relationship under examination here on a micro-level is one in which power resources are affected by the larger society and at the same time negotiated within each family group.

Power is usually analyzed macrosociologically: it cannot be solely a result of what people do within the immediate situation in which it occurs. What people do in specific interactions expresses and reflects historical and social structural forces beyond the boundaries of their encounters. . . . Power can, however, by analyzed microsociologically. . . . Power and hierarchical relations are not abstract forces operating on people. Power must be a human accomplishment, situated in everyday interaction. Both structural forces and interactional activities are vital to the maintenance and construction of social reality [Fishman, 1978: 397].

Using an exchange perspective to elucidate interaction in the "modified extended family," then, must take into account *both* broader social forces and negotiations within the family group.

The rewards that social actors offer one another vary in their incurred costs and the likelihood that they will be reciprocal. Blau (1964: 100) delineates six types of rewards available in social exchange in the schema shown in Table 1. Some rewards depend for their social value on being spontaneous. For example, the wealthy woman is skeptical of the poor suitor who maintains that he is "personally attracted" to her and may attribute calculation to his actions, thereby depriving them of social value. Others are expected to be calculated: rulers do not expect subjects to share incomes with them spontaneously out of respect.

Blau also makes a distinction between intrinsic rewards, those which are inherent in participating in relationships; extrinsic rewards, those which are available in relationships that serve as means to further ends; and unilateral rewards, those which depend for their value on subordination of the suppliers. In most discussions of exchange theory, family relationships are assumed to be intrinsically rewarding and

Table 1

	Intrinsic	Extrinsic	Unilateral
Spontaneous Evaluations	Personal attraction	Social approval[*]	Respect-prestige[+]
Calculated Actions	Social acceptance[*]	Instrumental services[*]	Compliance-power[+]

[*]Entails investment costs for suppliers in addition to those needed to establish the social association.

[+]Entails the direct cost of subordination for suppliers.

not well suited for analysis using this perspective. This may be valid for conjugal relationships, but for the old parent-offspring relationship the rewards evident in behavior are not limited to intrinsic rewards, but often fall under the unilateral heading and thereby entail "the direct cost of subordination."

Relationships in which one party is more dependent than the other on the particular relationship for rewards are described as "unbalanced."

> The variables appear to function jointly in fixing the dependence of one actor upon another. . . . The dependence of actor A upon actor B is (1) directly proportional to A's *motivational investment* in goals mediated by B, and (2) inversely proportional to the availability of those goals to A outside of the A-B relation [Emerson, 1962: 32].

In unbalanced relationships, one party has power over the other who is described as dependent.

For the old widow, rewards may be available from other sources, but circumstances change, usually in the direction of limiting the number of relationships available. Offspring may be the only source of acceptance, approval, and instrumental services. This is one of the primary features of an unbalanced relationship. While the likelihood of the old widow's offspring having other sources of these rewards is high, for example, from spouse, children, friends, or work associates, the old widow may depend only on the relationship for rewards. Her motivational investment in the relationship is high because the rewards from the relationship are both highly valued and seen as unavailable from any other source. The importance of maintaining the relationship is great, and explains the necessity of complying with the definition of her position in the family as handed down by her offspring.

Balancing Power

Emerson outlines four possible ways in which an unbalanced relationship may become balanced and the equality between actors restored or instituted. Blau (1964: 118) follows Emerson's lead, but reformulates his schema "to specify the conditions that produce imbalance of power itself." In order to avoid dependence on a particular relationship, a person must have at least one of these four options available: (1) access to strategic resources, (2) access to alternative sources of the desired reward, (3) some type of coercive force, (4) ability to do without the rewards available in the relationship. These methods for balancing may be used strategically or they may arise through fortuitous circumstances. When none of these options is taken, the less powerful party in the relationship must accept the unfavorable rate of exchange established by the more powerful partner.

If none of the four options for independence is available or acceptable to the old woman, she is forced to exchange subordination in the form of compliance or respect, or risk losing rewards in the relationship. These four alternatives are used by the old widows, but more often with the effect of gaining leverage rather than actually balancing power in the relationship. The four methods of balancing power as they are used by the informants are explained here. The labels attached to the methods are Blau's (1964: 124).

Supply inducements. The widow may supply her offspring with a service that is equal in value to the one she receives in exchange. These services will probably not be "in kind": the old widow is unlikely to be able to drive her offspring to a medical appointment in exchange for her offspring's driving her to a similar appointment. However, she may be able to provide an equally valuable service. For example, one old widow lives in an apartment complex which has a swimming pool. One of her granddaughters and her three great granddaughters visit often, especially in the summer. Another old widow has a cousin who together with his wife "have me over quite a lot."

> He is great on tradition, just great on family, but now there aren't any of us left. We're gone. He asked me some time ago to make a family tree. I'm the oldest, so I tell him and he writes it down.

In this particular relationship, the cousin's motivational investment in recording his family tree may be so high and the other sources of information so limited that the old woman has access to a particularly strategic resource. Although the old widow's social approval is not of great value in these relationships, she has other services which tend to balance power.

Fate may play a role in giving the old mother a position that includes rewards for exchange. One old widow lives near her son who is slightly disabled and divorced. She prepares at least one meal a day for him and does his laundry in exchange for his company and "moral support." Another old woman spent a great deal of time with her widowed daughter. Her son-in-law's death left a void that the old mother could fill. Indeed, old mothers living with their single, divorced, or widowed adult offspring is a fairly common occurrence (Siegel, 1972).

Obtain elsewhere. A second method of balancing power in the relationship is to find another person to provide the needed service or intrinsic rewards, thereby eliminating dependence on the relationship. Any public service designed to promote "independence" for the aged contributes to this power resource. Social security, old age assistance, and pensions provide the old with money that does not come from their offspring's coffers. Programs to aid the aged which are contingent on the amount that the aged person's relatives can contribute to his or her income have met with loud protests from the aged (Putnam, 1970). Relative responsibility clauses, by blatantly indicating financial dependence, undermine the power of the aged in relationships with offspring. Another service that contributes to power resources is efficient public or private transportation systems. Where these services are adequate and do not deflate self-images, they make asking relatives for transportation unnecessary. One old mother reported that her daughter-in-law offered to take her to the doctor "if she didn't have to work."

> I said, "Oh, I can get on the bus." I was mad, so I just said, "I can get on the bus." I have to go clear down to "A" Street between 1st and 2nd. But this lady next door will take me, I'm sure, if my daughter-in-law can't. She'd take me. She's very nice.

This old widow, by enlisting the services of her neighbor, will not be forced to comply with her daughter-in-law's time schedule. Another example is found in an old widow's relationship with her granddaughter. She and her daughter are not on particularly good terms. Her daughter's daughter, however, visits the old woman weekly to take her shopping and run other errands. The services for which she might be forced to depend on her daughter are provided by her granddaughter.

Take by force. A third alternative is coercion. The old woman may coerce the offspring to perform a needed service. Other than the rare old person who can threaten to withdraw financial support from her offspring, the only resource available is the inducement of guilt feelings that not performing the service will bring. This social currency becomes less valuable the more often it is used. Old widows' awareness of this is evident in the fact that they only expect to be supplied with "essential services" by their offspring: trips to their physicians and the grocery store, sometimes to church. These are all related to "life and death" matters. However, it is quite common among the informants to hear regrets about not being able to attend church services or lack of transportation to visit old friends who live five or ten miles away, usually a relatively easy trip by car, and a nightmare using public transportation. Offspring may be coerced through guilt to perform "important" services, but "less important" ones are too much of an imposition. Indeed, none of the informants complained specifically about her offspring's refusal to take her to visit friends. No one thought such a request appropriate.

A further instance of coercion, one that is not personally exercised by the old mother, but is to her advantage nonetheless, is found in belief systems that place importance on the extended family. An example of this is found in the beliefs and practices of the Mormon Church. One informant's two sons and granddaughter visit her each Monday evening for Bible study and family fellowship, a prescription of the church.

> My oldest son and his daughter come down every Monday evening and we have a . . . The Mormons have what you call a "family home evening." They believe in keeping the family together. But they come down every Monday evening and the four of us, we have such a nice time together. Have a social time, a little treat, and we also have a book that we're studying. We have a lesson. And, oh, I enjoy that so much. I just look forward to Mondays.

A belief in church doctrine, then, elevates this old woman's status and gives her legitimate power within her family.

Do without. A fourth possibility of balancing power in the relationship for the old widow is to resign herself to doing without the service. In this way her motivational investment is withdrawn and her offspring are no longer able to exercise power. Although many old widows would like to see their offspring more often and receive more services, they choose to be "independent," not to "bother" their children with everyday matters—in short, to do without desired rewards and goals. One informant spoke of her daughter:

She has a lot of friends, and a lot of company and I don't want to impose on her because her friends are younger, much younger than I am, of course. So I don't impose on her, only when I just have to.

In the language of social gerontologists, old women disengage, but not, as Cumming and Henry (1961) theorize, because it is inevitable. Rather, being engaged becomes increasingly costly as available resources usable in social exchange diminish. Compliance and respect are costly to self-esteem and are, therefore, not personally acceptable as social currency. Inducing offspring to provide transportation for seeing old friends, going to church, spending an evening on the town, is impossible when old women have few valuable resources to use as inducements. And so these activities, and hopes for them, are given up. Emotional investment is withdrawn.

"Doing without" is also descriptive of the behavior labeled "altruistic surrender" by Hochschild (1973: 98-111). One example Hochschild uses is that of the old mother whose daughter moved to a more expensive home. The old mother was jubilant about her daughter's good fortune even though it meant that she and her daughter would be separated by an additional hour and would not see each other as often. The old mother resigned herself to doing with "surprise" visits and daily telephone conversations with her child. Another choice might have been to complain bitterly and unhappily and thereby make the relationship more unbalanced in her offspring's favor. Further buttressing this argument is the fact that "surprise" visits by offspring to old mothers are seen as legitimate. However, the reverse is rarely true. Those with less power in the relationship must schedule meetings.

When Balancing Fails

This leads logically to the most common result of this imbalance of power, that is, compliance on the part of the dependent person with the wishes of the person with power over most aspects of the relationship. That compliance with the offspring's definition of the situation is a major response to the unbalanced relationship has already been discussed above in the review of the old widow's position in the family. The willingness of the aged to accept their children's behavior without criticism stems from lack of power in the relationship. If the old widow were critical or demanding, her behavior might legitimate overt rejection, and rejection and criticism by those who probably could not be replaced would be devastating to her self identity (Simmel, 1950: 122-128). Unfortunately the data can say nothing about how parent-adult offspring relationships change through time. The theory would predict that as the old mother's power resources diminish, she will become, at least overtly, more compliant and respectful of her offspring as her motivational investment in the relationship increases.

Evidence that old widows abide by decisions made for them by their offspring, sometimes at the expense of their own good judgment and wishes, is found in the following data.

> I was thinking of having one of the phones taken out, but Bob said no. They both have hearing aids in them. I can hear, but I can't distinguish the voices.

Although this informant wished to spend money on something other than a second phone, her son's wishes won out. Another old widow no longer drives at night.

> I drive, but I don't drive at night because the children said they didn't want me to feel that I might run out of gas or be struck by something. I just don't drive at night anymore. When I go out at night, someone calls for me. I thought that was the least I could do to ease their minds.

Another informant lamented the fact that she had no yard to work in at her present location.

Here I just rest. My son said, "You can't take care of a yard anymore." It's always, "We'll get you a little place," and that's where I am.

One old widow described her sister's unhappy plight. Her sister's husband had been placed in a rest home.

So it was really sad. She would go home and cry and cry and cry, and then she'd say, "I think I'll try to keep him." But the kids said, "No, you can't do that, Mother. You've tried it and you can't do it."

Although the woman involved here had a great deal of money, enough to pay for a live-in attendant, she still was unwilling to defy the decision made by her children. One informant, pleased by compliments of her roses, responded, "I wanted to get some more, but my daughter thought that six roses in that small bed was just plenty." Another informant said that she had recently told her children and grandchildren that she wished she could get in her old car and just go because she used to love to travel by car so much. In response to the query, "What did they say to that?" she replied:

Oh, they wouldn't be surprised. They usually let me do just about anything I want to, and try to get me to do some things I don't want to.

Another informant described her daughter:

She likes to tell me what I should do, and what I shouldn't do. I guess daughters are more or less that way. She thinks I ought to get out more, but I can't get out because I don't drive, you see, and have no way of getting out. And I don't take much pleasure in going to the market and back. There's no fun in that. So, I'm just kind of waiting. . . . When we were looking at places [for the informant to live], and we couldn't seem to find anything, and she was getting pretty tired out and she said, "I guess there are no more places. You'd better take this, Mother." So that was it.

It is important to emphasize that most of the informants cited here see their compliance as a personally acceptable resource to exchange for the approval and services of their offspring. Compliance is combined with respect and thereby seen as legitimate.

Some old widows cannot or will not add respect to their compliance which would make the situation personally acceptable. Bart (1975) has described these women as "The Portnoy's Mothers." One widow feels trapped by the power-dependency relationship, but sees no alternative to complying with her son and daughter-in-law's decisions. Her comments show clearly the lack of power in the relationship:

I don't mind her coming. What makes me mad is her giving me orders what to do and what not to do. . . . Would you like it? Have your kids telling you what to do?

I never fail to say thank you to Linda. This morning she rattled the door and said, "Here's your morning paper, Millie." "Thank you." And I have to remember to always thank her for everything. If I don't she wears a distressed look on her face.

She comes over here once in a while when she gets some of her cockeyed notions—she doesn't like the way I've got the bathroom or something. One day she came in and I said, "I want to wash my windows. I think I can do it, but it would be nice to have someone on the inside and someone on the outside." So I said, "I'll do the inside and you'll do the outside." So she came over here on Sunday and said, "Sit down over there, Millie," and she just took over. I said to someone one day, "I don't live here, you know. Linda lives here."

Inability or unwillingness to see as legitimate power holders those with whom she must comply makes dependency obvious and damaging to self-identity.

Open defiance of offsprings' expectations is rare, but more subtle acts of noncompliance occur. One common act of defiance is to wait until a controversial decision is a fait accompli before announcing it to offspring. One old woman who had moved from a home she had occupied for 42 years located near a small town to a 15-acre ranch on top of a mountain, explained:

> I had a big row with my kids, especially my oldest daughter. She didn't want me to move up here. But I didn't tell her anything about it 'til I got all the papers and everything. Why let your kids tell you what to do [Fran et al., 1974]?

At the same time this woman recognizes that her power resources may diminish. "When I get crippled up so I can't wait on myself, then they can tell me what to do." Another woman has moved several times within the small community in which she lives. Each time she has completed all the arrangements, overcoming the anticipated objections, before informing her daughter whose objections had already been overruled.

A second method of covert noncompliance is to play the role of an "old lady." In using this strategy, the old woman gains leverage in situations by consciously adopting the attributes others may assume she has because she is old.

> My daughter-in-law is a pest. Last time I went [to the doctor] she had to take me because I didn't have anyone else. She told the doctor, "I want her ears washed out. She doesn't hear anything I say." I whispered to him and I said, "Well, I'll tell you why. She says a lot of things I don't want to hear and I just turn off." She accused me of it one time. "You just turn off when you don't want to hear something." That's what I do.

Thus, the old woman gains control over her disliked daughter-in-law by playing the role of the deaf old lady. She even seems to get some satisfaction out of her daughter-in-law's not knowing whether she is acting or not. Another woman described a situation in which her son had asked if she would like to take home some leftover turkey:

> I said, "Why, yes." [very sweetly] I think my daughter-in-law is mad because he gave me all the turkey. If I'd been her, and he

was there giving me all that turkey, I'd have thrown a leg at him. [laughter] He was giving it to good old grandmother.

There is a widely held notion that old people are to be envied because they are no longer constrained by social norms. Surprisingly, perhaps, this advantage of being old is rarely expressed overtly by the informants and when it is it may be brought to the old person's attention. One old woman described a funny situation she had gotten herself into in a bar.

I was telling this [young] friend up here about it and she said, "You make me mad. You're just old enough that you can do all those things and get away with it."

Examples of this are rare. In order to use this strategy, the old woman must admit to herself that she is being treated badly by someone, that someone has a different image of her than she has of herself, which undermines maintenance of self-identity.

The Meaning of Family Membership

In sociology the family is most often discussed in terms of its functions for society (regulation of sexual behavior and the socialization of new members of society) and its importance in placing individuals relative to other members of society (kinship structures and social class differences) [cf. Coser, 1975]. This is the perspective from which Parsons (1942) theorized that the nuclear family, rather than the extended family, is both economically and socially the family type best suited for industrial societies.

An alternative perspective for analyzing the role of the family is from the point of view of family members, especially its adult members. This is, in part, the perspective Litwak (1960) takes when he defines the "modified extended family," stressing, in addition to its functions for society, that its members see the bonds between them as intrinsically valuable. This perspective is also taken by Ryder (1974) when he observes that, "The conjugal family serves as an oasis for the replenishment of the person, providing the individual with stable, diffuse, and largely unquestioning support." Goode (1963) speaks from both perspectives, pointing out the function of the family for society and for family members.

> Goode's analysis of the evolving functions of the family in industrialized societies points to the unique "fit" between the affectively based conjugal unit and the achievement oriented society. He notes that the conjugal family is uniquely suited to provide the psychological and emotional support individuals need to deal with the industrial system's focus on impersonal individual achievements. Because the conjugal system lays great emphasis on the emotional solace its members give to one another, the family becomes the place where the individual tensions and the emotional imbalance of industrial participation are somewhat redressed [Weitzman, 1974: 1199].

Clark and Anderson (1967) also found a similar meaning of the conjugal relationship for old couples, whose relationship with one another is seen as more egalitarian and important than it was in middle age. With the exception of Litwak and Sussman, all these authors are speaking of the nuclear or conjugal family. This research, however, focuses on the old mother who is a widow and, therefore, no longer a partner in a conjugal relationship. Does being an old widowed mother in an "extended family" also provide psychological and emotional support to older members who are no longer in conjugal relationships?

The evidence presented here indicates that the answer is "no." The "moral support" available to the old widowed mother is qualitatively different from that available to those in ideal conjugal relationships. The data indicate that the extended family structure is intact, but that the quality of the relationships is affected adversely by the low status of old women who have a weak power base from which to demand to be treated as equals. They are dependent on the relationship because in their eyes they have no one else to whom to turn for "moral support."

Lack of Power Resources in the Sacred Institution

The strategies used by the informants in an attempt to balance power are familiar ones. Indeed, the terms used to label the strategies are generic and not specific to old widows. Few social actors are lucky enough, or tyrannical enough, to wield power without being forced to respect those whom they expect to comply with their wishes. All groups, even two-person groups, are structured so that some members have power over others with respect to given resources, and desired resources are often scarce. Graduate students, for example, and others training for professional careers, are left with few choices but to comply with the rules set down by their professors, unless they are geniuses. However, even genius may go unrecognized if the student goes "too far"; "too far" being defined by those in power, and the pathway to a desired career blocked. What is unusual in the situation described here is that, because it deals with the family, there are a dearth of available alternatives for reaching desired goals.

Old widowed mothers are not alone in their mismatch with the ideal of familial psychological and emotional support. The prototype, of course, are children who, first because of their size and second because of overwhelming social-structural forces, are tied to biological parents who literally have the power of life and death over them (Taylor, 1971). Adopted, deserted, battered, and "culturally deprived" children are in situations similar to old widowed mothers, in that within the family institution they have a weak power base from which to successfully negotiate relationships that are to their disadvantage. Women have also suffered from lack of available alternatives to participation in marriage and family formation.

The family is a sacred institution and failure to be a member of a loving, intact, stable family is seen and often accepted as personal failure. Many members of society survive very well outside intact families (Gubrium, 1975). However, their personal survival is probably hindered by the belief that the family is all important (Keller, 1971). This belief has been firmly institutionalized in social welfare legislation that is based on "hands off" policies with respect to the internal workings of family groups as well as in the discrepancy in monetary rewards between "men's occupations" and "women's work."

Failure to belong to a supportive family, then, may have very serious personal and social consequences. If an old widow is rejected by her family, to whom does she turn for "moral support?" If a child finds living with his or her parents and siblings intolerable, where can s/he go to escape? S/he may see viable alternatives, but those with power will probably reject them in favor of returning him or her to the nuclear family setting. If a woman chooses to be a single parent she may face real problems in commanding a large enough income to support her children.

This analysis of the old widowed mother's position in the extended family indicates that past emphasis on the extended family structure being alive and well has hidden the qualitative nature of family relationships for old mothers and has painted a more rosey picture than is justified. Perhaps the time has come to investigate successful methods of gaining "moral support" from relationships and to promote them rather than assuming that the family is the most appropriate source of such support. Indeed, there is a possibility that more and more people will take the option not to have children, thereby severely limiting the number of persons to whom they are biologically related, and the importance of biological relatedness will diminish.

NOTES

1. I am grateful to Gordon F. Lewis and J. Timothy Diamond for suggesting revisions on earlier drafts of this paper. Shortcomings that remain must be attributed to the author.

2. As an example of "typical survey questions," the cross-cultural research conducted by Shanas et al. (1968), based on samples drawn from the United States, Great Britain, and Denmark, draws conclusions about old parent-offspring relationships based on the following:

1. The number of living children, number of sons and daughters.
2. For each child: sex, marital status, proximity to the home of the old person, time of last contact.
3. Help given to and received from children.
4. Help from children (among others) in a number of specific situations, such as household activities, shopping during illness, etc. [Shanas et al., 1968: 181].

3. Increased leisure time from the actor's perspective is usually a cost. Blau (1964: 101) points out that "The most general cost incurred in supplying any social reward is the time required to do so in social associations . . . the significance of this time depends on the alternatives foregone by devoting it to a given exchange relation." For example, when I expressed concern about keeping an old couple waiting to a medical professional, he said it did not matter. They were retired and didn't have anything to do but sit around home any way. Increasing available time decreases its value as a resource in social exchange.

Chapter 7

CONFRONTING THE GRIM REAPER

A basic tenet of symbolic interactionism is that persons in the process of becoming human gain self-consciousness by taking on the attitudes of others toward their own bodies, actions, and thoughts.[1] Biological humans become persons and have selves when they are able to see themselves as both the subject and object of situations. In Mead's terms, they possess a self composed of the "I," the participant in each moment of the day, and the "me," the attitudes of others adopted to preview and judge their own participation (Mead, 1970: 135-226). In preparing to act, humans mentally rehearse actions to assess the possible meanings and gage others' reactions to them in order to project and maintain the image they have of themselves (Goffman, 1959).

In most situations, persons are engaged in the process of ascertaining the symbolic significance of their actions to themselves and others. In situations which have not been

accomplished, which are in the planning stage, the participating self, the "I," cannot be known absolutely. People plan
for future acts, but "the real self that appears in that act
awaits the completion of the act itself" (Mead, 1970: 203).
Even so, most people are able to plan for the future with
reasonable confidence and, except in stressful situations,
rarely question their ability to maintain a personally acceptable self-image.

For old people the prospect of physical and mental infirmity, dependence and death looms ever larger with each
passing year, making problematic their ability to project and
maintain a desired self-image in the future. At this point in
history in this society death is something that "naturally"
happens to old people.

> Whatever the complex problems of the roles this group of "old-
> sters" are to assume or have already assumed, they are a group
> who, by the nature of their position in the society are "living in
> the shadow of death," since they have entered what is by all
> institutional criterion, a terminal period of their lives" [Parsons,
> 1963: 62].

The actual dying process, with all its unknowns, may mean
that the old person will be in situations in which s/he will be
a participant and at the same time be unable to participate in
negotiating the definitions of those situations. For this person there will be no "signs given," only "signs given off"
(Goffman, 1959: 2), and these will be signs over which the
dying (or dead) participant has little or no control.

Old people, then, are faced with the possibility in the
unknowable future (and in the knowable future, since death
is inevitable), of situations in which they will be unable to
present themselves as the persons they "really are," situations
in which projecting their own views of themselves, their
self-identities, may be out of their control. This is the problematic situation addressed in the analysis that follows. This
concept of uncertainty will be presented first, followed by a

discussion of the strategies employed to eliminate the uncertainty and maintain a desired self-identity in dying and death.

Death and Uncertainty

The basic uncertainty of the how and when of death is a recurrent topic of conversation among old women. Although death is often considered a "taboo topic" by sociologists (Cowgill, 1972), and Cumming and Henry (1961: 63) found that only a tiny fraction of their sample admitted thinking about death and dying, Hochschild (1973: 79) in a participant observation study of a senior citizens housing project found that death "was a fact of life in Merrill Court and there was no taboo against talking about it." Ross (1977) and Marshall (1975) report similar findings in the retirement communities they studied. This was also true of the informants for this research.

That death cannot be definitively planned for is mentioned often by old people in a variety of ways. For example, one old woman told of a birthday party for a woman in her sewing club:

> And you know that night that woman passed away. Died in her sleep. We were all just sick about it. She had been quite well for the last few years. She'd had heart trouble. The next day one of her friends called to tell me and I said, "Why I can't believe it." I remember the last thing she said. She came over to where I was sewing and said goodbye. We had had such a wonderful lunch. We had a beautiful cake for her. Honestly, you know, we're here today and gone tomorrow.

Another old woman pointed out that there is no logic that will predict time of death, even when it appears that there might be.

> There's another widow up here. Her husband was at the prison for years and he retired. And they were both kind of sickly, but

she was more sickly than he, and yet he passed away and she's still here. You never know, do you? He seemed like to go so sudden.

One informant explained to the interviewer:

That's what I say about your mother. You don't know what will happen. You don't know. You can't live but today. Yesterday's gone, and tomorrow's hearsay. You don't know what will happen to your mother. She may die over night with a heart attack and she may live to be one hundred and three. You don't know.

Other references to the uncertainty with which old people are faced is evident in conversations such as the following:

First of July, if I live, first of July I was married sixty-five years.

If anything happens to me [before the trip] you'll give the money to my son won't you? We never know what might happen. You'll read about it in the paper. You'll know if something happens to me.

I haven't been to Las Vegas since my oldest boy was two years old. I'm going to go next year. [Slight pause] If I'm still here.

I want to live to see him when he's ninety.

When death will occur, then, cannot be predicted and, therefore, cannot be taken into account when planning for the future. One old woman summed up her thoughts on death in a statement that is representative of old women generally:

Why should I worry about that? It's something everybody has to accept, but I'm not looking forward to it.

Death may be taken as inevitable and not worth worrying about, but the process of dying is another matter entirely. The events that will precede death, again, cannot be predicted, but old women can plan in order to maintain their self-identities during the dying process. Fear of the dying process centers on "suffering" and "being a burden," both of which fall under the category of losing control over self-identity.

> I'm not in a hurry to die because I feel like I've still got quite a bit to accomplish here. I'm not afraid of death itself, but I'm afraid of pain. I have a fear of lingering. That I don't want to do. I don't want to have to be taken care of. I've been active all my life and taken care of myself and I just don't want anybody to have to take care of me. Not a fear of death, but a fear of being probably in a wheel chair and having a stroke and having to lie in bed or in a rest home.

The old women, then, did not fear death per se, which they saw as inevitable and unpredictable. Their fears centered on the dying process itself and the possibility that they would die "badly," that is, that they would linger and lose control of their selves.

Strategies for Controling Dying

There are various strategies that the old woman uses to control self-identity during the dying process. She, of course, cannot be certain that she will be able to maintain control over her self and social identities, but she may use strategies that make potential loss of control less uncertain.

Monitoring Warning Signals

For the old woman a visit to the doctor takes on new meaning—it becomes a safeguard against lingering. The strategy here is to watch carefully the signs that are associated with a long dying process, and thereby avoid one. One old woman goes to her doctor regularly even though she is in "pretty good shape."

> I do go for checkups and high blood pressure, you know. You've got to watch that when you get over seventy. You watch because

that's the time when you're more likely to have a stroke or something like that. That's one thing I have a screaming horror of, is being disabled and lay around for years disabled. But that's God's will. We can't say, but I do watch my blood pressure on account of [my mother-in-law died of a stroke, my father-in-law died of a stroke] and we'll say indirectly my husband died of a stroke. And I know what it's all about. If they had watched their blood pressure and their diet when they found out it was high. . . .

Other activities are also performed as a way of increasing the likelihood that lingering can be avoided. One informant forced herself to take a daily walk in order to avoid being crippled by arthritis. Another woman said that she had played bridge three days in succession and gone to a church meeting the day before, so she was "laying off for the rest of the week to balance it off," to avoid a heart attack. She had had one twelve years earlier.

There appears to be a belief by the old woman that if she monitors her body very carefully, she will increase the probability that she will live longer than she would otherwise and that when she dies, she will go quickly.

Symbolic Maintenance of Self-Identity

Planning in advance for the division of property and for funeral arrangements is another way to maintain self-identity while dying and dead. Possessions that are valuable to the old woman may be viewed as "ego-involvements" (Shibutani, 1961: 224), in that they become experienced as part of the old woman herself, and as such can be used symbolically in interaction with others. She can plan a distribution of her possessions so that everyone who is important to her knows how she feels about him or her, even when she no longer has control over her self-identity. The concern with who gets what, then, appears to be not so much with living on in her possessions after her death, as is often assumed, but with maintaining an image of herself that she sees as acceptable when she is no longer in control of herself. For example one old woman said:

> I hate to leave little Christy [granddaughter]. That [china] is all for Christy after I've gone.

The same goal is attained in distributing goods while she is still of sound mind and body:

> I've given all my good things and dishes to my granddaughter. I dearly love her.

Another informant was in the process of carefully making a list of her possessions and dividing them equitably between her two granddaughters. Her concern was not so much that her possessions have good homes, but that her relatives see her as fair and benevolent. Thus, by planning very carefully in advance, she felt she would be maintaining her image of herself even when she would no longer be here.

One old woman wished to convey a very different message to her relatives. She sends her grandson five dollars every Saturday: "That way when the vultures come around there won't be anything left." The following description of how one old woman plans her funeral is a message to her daughter with whom she has a less than ideal relationship:

> I've joined that Memorial thing and I'm just going to fix it so that they come over and pack me up and take me over and cremate me. For years I hated the idea of cremation. It seemed so unnatural. Putting your body back in the earth and letting it do what it could to feed back seemed more natural. Since I'm old, it would just seem sensible to get it over in twenty-four hours. The first time this happened to my friends, it just seemed monstrous to me, to take a body that was still warm and put it in the crematorium. But after all, what does it matter? Just save her [daughter] having to make a decision. And it's so expensive. . . . Why go to the expense? Burials have become so expensive. Fifteen hundred dollars to plant a body is kind of ridiculous

today. I realized after my mother died, and I wished I'd realized it before. If you're going to give flowers to people, do it while they can still smell them. The time to say I love you is when they can still respond, because there is no response in a dead body. She will do what she pleases. I think my daughter is motivated by a lot of fear. I think my daughter is scared to death of an awfully lot of things.[2]

By planning for an impersonal cremation, this old woman will be symbolically interacting with her "irresponsible" daughter, using the disposition of her body to maintain her own view of herself and her daughter in the distressing relationship. Most incidents of this strategy are less overt and are found in such statements as, "My children know what I want." Thus, she has designated others to maintain her self-image when it is no longer in her control.

Planning for Sudden Physical Malfunction

One constant source of uncertainty for the old woman is not knowing when or where her body will fail her. The fear of being completely helpless and no one being aware of the fact is voiced often.[3]

I don't know what I would do in the night, if I were to have a stroke or something and couldn't get to the telephone.

She deals with this potential dilemma by making arrangements with a neighbor on the other side of the wall. "All I have to do is knock." Or as another informant explained:

What worries me is when you live alone, and when you get older, you don't know when death will strike. You might be alone, might have sort of a heart attack when you're alone, and you could be alone for two or three days before anyone would know. That's the part that bothers me. Anne always calls me up at nine in the morning and I always manage to be here so I won't worry her. I'm quite sure that if I didn't answer and she tried and tried. . . . We have a sort of plan like that.

The image of herself suffering and being unable to call for help is frightening, but the image of herself being dead and no one taking note of her passing is also frightening and threatening to her sense of self. By carefully arranging her daily rounds, she is able to minimize the possibility of being in a completely helpless condition or dead for a long period of time without anyone knowing. Another old woman is fearful of where her body will suddenly fail her:

> Everytime I go out on the street, I think of this: If I should collapse. In this city I don't know anybody anymore. I used to know about everybody who lived here years and years ago. Now I don't know anybody and they don't know me. And I always think if I should collapse I have a horror of that medical center out there. I have a horror of that place. The County Hospital it used to be. And I think, if I should collapse, that's where they'll cart me, out there, and I have such a horror of it. I think about that a lot.

She deals with this uncertainty by carrying a card with her that has her doctor's name on it, "So that might help." Like other old people, this woman lives with the fear that she will suddenly become a body to be "carted" instead of the "person" she is.

One atypical old woman confronts the uncertainty surrounding the dying process by adopting an ideology that eliminates uncertainty.

> I think probably as you grow older your will to survive is not so great. . . . I think there ought to be euthanasia. Is there any point to lingering on until you are totally incapacitated? What's so wonderful about life? It's the quality of life, not the quantity. I would much rather choose to die than to live with cancer or stroke or heart condition.

And in "choosing" she will eliminate potential lack of control over her self-identity.

For the old woman, the unknowable circumstances surrounding a potential malfunction of the body are taken into account and planned for so that their effect on her self and social identity may be minimized and at least some of the felt precariousness of her situation diminished.

Taking the Unknowable Into Account

Everyone must deal with situations on which the unknowable may impinge, although most everyday situations are assumed to be knowable and predictable. Social actors are rarely "surprised." Humans have a propensity for turning the unusual into the routinized. Some situations, like the how and when of death, cannot be known, but social actors attempt to turn the unknowable into the predictable, to find order where there is none. The timing of death and the events surrounding it are not the only unknowns with which social actors must deal. Most belief systems which "explain" the unknowable fall under the rubric of religion or magic: rituals are performed which seem to make predictable the unknowable. Many acts are performed, however, whose consequences are within the forseeable future.

To cite a frivolous example, greengrocer Joe Carcione maintains that choosing a good watermelon is based on luck and only on luck. However, even shoppers who admit that they are at a loss in choosing a watermelon can be seen carefully examining and thumping before making purchases, and many willingly share with fellow thumpers their proven techniques. Randomness appears to be made predictable. There are many patternless events in everyday life for which people make up explanations and the fabrications are born out in fact because the events would occur regardless: most children grow up whether parents are lax or strict disciplinarians; most watermelons are edible.

Accepting unconditionally that some things cannot be known seems to be an impossibility for most social actors. Examinations of past events in order to predict future events, to make the future at least a little more certain, is a very common occurrence. Old women who face imminent death are certainly not exceptions to this general rule.

Ignoring the work of the Grim Reaper becomes increasingly difficult as one year makes way for the next and gradually lengthens each person's accumulated time on earth. For old people, death, and the period of time preceding it, comes inevitably closer, and the prospect of being physically dependent on someone and of no longer being an active participant in social life become possibilities that are taken into account. This analysis has dealt with ways in which old women attempt to make the dying process less uncertain—with few ambiguities that could be interpreted inaccurately and be damaging to the self-images they wish to project.

Death itself is faced with resignation.[4] One old woman summed up the situation, "I guess everybody's life is different and you just have to live on until you're taken. There's nothing you can do about it." At the same time, death and the dying process are not seen as the end of the self, but as situations requiring careful planning to maintain the person that the old woman sees herself to be. The women who supplied the data for this analysis would agree with de Beauvoir (1972: 441) as she contemplates her own death.

> I shall be dead for others, not for myself: it is the Other who is mortal in my being. I know that I am mortal, just as I know that I am old, by adopting the outsider's view of me. This knowledge is therefore abstract, general, and assumed from without. My "mortality" is in no way the object of any close, inward experience. I am not unaware of it; in practical life I take it into account in my plans and my decisions, in so far as I treat myself as an Other: but I do not *feel* it.

NOTES

1. This chapter appeared in slightly different form in *Urban Life* 4(3): 339-348 (1975).

2. The informant's discussion of her corpse is unusual. Hochschild (1973: 84-85) found that, "Although the widows talked about the events leading up to death and death itself frankly, in detail, and even in a matter-of-fact way, they seldom mentioned what happened to the body afterward. It is as if the taboo that for young people stops before death, is for old people, moved beyond it.... Although death was not considered depressing, the use of one's physical remains was."

3. The informants who furnished the data for this analysis are all widows living alone. Old women who live with spouses and in households with other people, or in apartment houses equipped with emergency call buttons and lights, may not see sudden physical malfunctions as problematic. Unfortunately, the resolution of this issue lies outside the scope of the data.

4. Becker (1962: 70) writes most eloquently of the resignation with which death is faced. "The self is a symbolic fiction which throbs with experience that mere flesh and blood could never relay. The self trails its body into old age, after a lifetime of daily scrutiny in a mirror, of a biological aging process it does not understand. Approaching death, the magnificent, intricate, symbolic creation of history—the self—can show only resignation. For the self-reflexive animal, death is an absurd injustice, which thousands of years and unnumbered systems of thought have labored to explain."

Chapter 8

NEGOTIATING IDENTITY IN A SETTING

The analysis would be incomplete if left at this micro-level. Too often research within a social interactionist framework is one-sided, and the preceding analysis of the informants' social worlds is no exception in that it has relied only on the old widows' definitions of the problematic situations. In fact, identity maintenance is a process of negotiation. In this chapter, maintenance of self-identity is brought into sharper focus through analysis of the interaction between staff and participants in the senior center in which I was a participant observer. Recent social legislation affecting the social position of the aged will be discussed in light of the precarious nature of the self-identities of the old widows. The argument will be made that the Older Americans Act has defined old age as postadulthood and set in place a group of "gerontologized" professionals and quasi-professionals who promote this social image of the old.[1] A senior center staffed by these new professionals who minister to the old is a setting in which the clash between the social identity and the self-identity of the old must be actively confronted.

The Institutionalization of Postadulthood

To review the argument made in Chapter 2, the Social Security legislation of the 1930s was based on the assumed incapacity of old persons to function as adult members of society, but the assumption was only implicit. The Social Security Act and, later, Medicare both attended officially to the financial position of old persons. The Older Americans Act of 1965, however, officially legislated old-age itself to be a problem, not merely limited income. The process that began in the 1930s when retirement and a retirement age were instituted on a broad scale has finally culminated in the institutionalization of a postadult period in the life cycle in which persons past retirement age are officially considered incapable of dealing effectively with their own lives. At the same time, the Act called for the creation of a network of people who would actively promote this image of the old.

The Older Americans Act has had little effect on the income of the elderly, but, rather, has made resources available to "middleman programs," that is, programs that "fund and empower public and private organizations to develop and operate properties and carry out services" (Binstock, 1972: 271). Money, then, does not go to the old, but to people paid "to help" the old deal with their "unmet needs." Adult members of society may have unmet needs,[2] but are generally thought capable of dealing with them unless for some other reason they are viewed as incompetent, for example, because of "mental illness" or immersion in a "culture of poverty." The old, however, simply because of their age, are deemed incapable. In essence, they are assumed to be "postadults." Many of the people who benefit most directly from this "war on old age" quite naturally are most interested in the problems of securing additional funds to expand their programs and in justifying the programs that are already in existence. I am not suggesting that these workers are motivated purely be self-interest or that they do not have the best interest of "the elderly" at heart. What I am suggesting is that these workers, in order to justify their positions, must see the aged as postadults and, in doing their jobs, promote a view of the aged as postadults.

As the above analysis makes clear, most of the old are not so compliant as to adopt this definition for themselves. Rather they assert that they are middle-aged, not old. To define oneself as middle-aged is to think of oneself as an independent social actor, an adult member of society. To reject a self-designation of old is to reject the notion that advanced chronological age makes one only marginally fit for adult status in society. If, in fact, the social definition of the old promoted by the gerontological professionals is in opposition to the self-definition held by the old, strategies to protect self-image might be expected to be used by the old in a senior citizens center in which representatives of the two groups interact.

The Senior Citizens Center: The Staff's View

Senior citizens centers are conceived of and actively promoted as places in which the old meet to engage with one another in a variety of activities as well as places where services can be dispensed. In the Center in which I was employed, there was a supervisor of senior citizens programs, a part-time social worker in charge of information and referral, a full-time transportation coordinator/bus dirver, a half-time activities coordinator, and two receptionists who shared the full-time job. In the summer months, a high school student also joined the staff and there were occasional college students helping with various projects such as a "needs assessment survey." The more successful a center is at securing federal, state, and local funds, the larger the number of social service delivery workers that can be directly employed. In addition to the regular staff, representatives of various services appeared weekly, monthly, or annually to discuss or provide services. For example, a representative of the Housing Authority, someone who gave hearing tests, a Social Security representative, someone from legal aid, and an income tax consultant appeared periodically.

Most of the staff at the Center promoted a social definition of old age as postadulthood. The supervisor's view of his role in the community was "not so much to develop programs but to develop a community sense of involvement with the problems of older citizens of the town." On another occasion, he explained to a group of disgruntled participants, "I see myself having an office with a phone and a part-time secretary. I'm supposed to be coordinating your needs—transportation, health and employment services." In a letter addressed to organizations in the community and county, he stated, "There are more than 4,000 senior citizens in the area that the other citizens of our community do not know about." In a subsequent letter addressed to the same audience, he wrote:

> Older persons, especially those who are ill, poor, or otherwise disadvantaged, are "invisible" citizens of the community. We need your help in finding these people and we are eager to help you care for their many needs.

Or again, he stated that his purpose was "to develop talent in the seniors to take over the program." As will be seen below, a number of the "seniors" felt that their talents were already sufficiently developed.

It is critical for this analysis that the rhetoric used here not be passed over lightly. Edelman (1977: 68) has pointed out that professionals, and laypersons who *want* to trust them,

> respond partly to the *forms* of language, as predetermined by the categories and observational methods of the profession. These

forms evoke perceptions and beliefs that are all the more potent because they are subtly and often unconsciously expressed and understood.

It is therefore important to make explicit the assumptions about the old that lie behind the supervisor's words. The picture of the old that these words produce is of persons who by virtue of their age no longer have physical or social resources with which to tackle the myriad of supposedly unique problems facing them. They need "help" and the language of help implies that the old most be located, cared for, and directed "for their own good" (Edelman, 1977). Old people require the help of professionals who know best how to organize their lives for them so that their needs, which they as old people are incapable of recognizing, might be met. The alternative, supposedly the only alternative, is to be isolated and invisible.

The rhetoric was put into action by the staff at the senior center. The Center was seen by those paid to staff it as a place where old people could come to escape isolation by participating in planned activities as well as a place where social services specifically tailored to their needs would be available. The staff, however, sometimes openly, more often covertly, treated the old people who came to the Center as people they need not interact with as adults. Almost by definition, if they came to the Center, if they needed or wanted the services provided there, they relinquished their status as adult members of society in the eyes of the staff.

Perhaps the most blatant example of the nonadult status attributed to the participants by staff occurred during the monthly potluck of one of the organizations that met at the Center. The president of the club called for silence and began making announcements. Staff who had been invited to join continued to talk in normal voices until they were finally "shushed" by the old people next to whom they were sitting.

Another example of nonadult status attributed to participants occurred when an unhappy old woman came in to discuss changing her will with the social worker. The social worker later called the old woman's daughter and was satisfied that she was "taking responsibility." He had told the old woman "to consult her banker for the name of a lawyer" and hoped she would "forget about it before she [could] do anything." No referral to the legal aid representative was made. On another occasion he advised the bus driver, "Oh, they [passengers] are never wrong. You should never argue with them or tell them they're wrong." In essence, his advice was to discourage personal responsibility and independence and to encourage "spurious feedback" (Lemert, 1967).[3]

Knowledge of the political scene in the community was defined by the supervisor as too strategically valuable to share openly with the participants at the Center. The supervisor had a great deal of knowledge about budgets and city council decisions that were political rather than rational. When participants at the Center planned strategies to influence city council members, the information would have been very helpful. It was withheld. The old people were viewed as enemies rather than allies. When the participants attempted to plan serious actions they were often plotted against or ridiculed behind closed doors. For example, the supervisor, commenting on a business meeting of one of the clubs, said to a staff member, "You should hear them out there. They've appointed the whole Commission. They've got fifteen names to recommend already. I've been eating my lunch and listening, trying to keep from having hysterics."

The Senior Citizens Advisory Board, composed primarily of old people, most of whom had high status in the community but rarely participated in Center activities, was viewed as ineffective. They had no specific role and lacked strategic information. The Board was merely a "token," a requirement of the granting agency. On one occasion the city manager apologized to the Board for not having submitted the senior citizens budget to the Board before sending it to the recreation committee. Only after meeting with the Board did she realize she was bypassing not only adults, but adults with high status in the community.

Activities at the Center planned by the staff often had as their implicit purpose getting people together to fill their supposedly empty, lonely hours with activities. The supervisor explained: "We want not only to liberate seniors from watching television but also to get them involved with other people and in the community." The main purpose of the exercise class, for example, as described by a staff member, was to "improve the seniors' physical condition while they enjoy the companionship of others." One current events discussion group was begun merely to get the leader of the group involved. Several people attended the first meeting, but the leader who was being "allowed" to volunteer his services was almost completely deaf. No one showed up for the second meeting.

Perhaps the best example of the underlying purpose of plans was the ill-fated "needs assessment survey":

> Originally, members of the Senior Advisory Board had planned to conduct a door-to-door two page questionnaire survey this fall of the community's senior citizens. Last night, however, a subcommittee of the advisory board decided they wanted to "create rapport and warmth for the program within the community."[4]

The supervisor of senior citizens programs and the staff at the Center, through their words and actions, defined old people as postadults incapable of meeting their own needs, who, without extensive services and planned activities would live in social isolation. Estes (1973: 182) writes:

> We know that the elderly, just like everyone else, operate on the basis of meanings which are derived from and modified by the interactions they have with others in their environment. If in there interactions, old people encounter negative perceptions held by others of them, they will undoubtedly come to share similar negative perceptions of themselves.

Old people, however, are not merely reactors to others' imputations of them. They are actors capable of actions of their own.

The Senior Citizens Center: Participants' Views

Participants in Center activities did not consider themselves to be "typical" old people. One participant stated:

> When the supervisor came to town to take the job he found people who weren't really considered "senior citizens." The people he met didn't need his services. After all, there aren't any migrant laborers here. There just aren't the problems here with old people that there are in other communities. This community's old people are a different breed.

Her analysis of the situation clearly shows the clash between imputed attributes and self-identity. To protect self-identity in the setting the old people used two strategies, confrontation and role distance.

Confrontation

Before federal funds were made available to hire a supervisor of senior citizens programs and a senior center was established by the city, there had been a social club, composed primarily of old widows, that met regularly. This social group was "sponsored" by the recreation department which had hired a part-time coordinator to assist it. Club members and their coordinator were instrumental in the process of applying for funds and viewed the newly established Center as their territory, a clubhouse in which to continue and expand their activities. There was, then, a group with strong and vocal leadership already in place who resented the post-adult status that was ascribed to them. Choosing a site for the Center and determining who would in fact be in charge of the activities there was an issue from the start. One member stated the case:

We are adults and would like to at least be consulted before changes are made in our constitution. We are grown people and can make our own decisions. I think guidelines should be established for the director. I don't believe he has asked us on any of these activities. We just want our own building so we can organize our own programs. We are willing to help him but we do not want our authority taken away from us.

Another member of the club echoed the above sentiments: "It's as if people who run things in this town don't trust us. . . . They think we're beyond the age of imagination and competence." Or again, "We are not sheep with him [the supervisor] as our shepherd. We're not senile. We want to be consulted about projects that involve us." One club member suggested changing the job title from supervisor to coordinator: "We don't need any supervision."

In order to maintain or regain control over the programming of senior activities in town, the club members used several strategies. The club voted to change its name from the "50-Plus Club" to "Senior Citizens of Columbia." The president explained that "the name-change is a 'clarification' of the senior club's official position in the city." The name-change was accompanied by an active recruitment effort. The club grew from a group of less than fifty to a group of over 300, at least on paper. Membership fees were minimal and accurate records were kept so that on any given day the president could state exactly how many people he represented. The generic term "senior citizen" became the specific name of the club so that in conversations, newspaper articles, and publicity, there was some question about whether the activity was being sponsored by the club or the Center.

Often the club would quickly carry through a proposal made by the staff or the Advisory Board. For example, the Board discussed issuing cards that could be used by senior citizens to get discounts at particular stores or theatres. The club president arranged to have cards printed and distributed to the membership almost immediately.

Another key effort to maintain or regain autonomy was to mount a campaign to remove the Advisory Board from the recreation department to give it direct access to the city council. This was a move that was also sponsored by the Advisory Board, but for a very different reason. The Board was interested in moving so that it would serve the function of dealing with all the "unmet needs" of the elderly, not merely recreation needs. The chair of the Advisory Board stated, "We need to move away from the recreation relationship. With the seriousness of the problems senior citizens are facing we need to meet all the needs of the seniors." The club, however, felt that direct access to the city council gave them a public forum in which their requests were more likely to be granted. Going through the recreation department had often resulted in unkept promises and run-arounds. Appearing before the city council, however, allowed the club members to fill the council chambers to demonstrate support. An analysis of the minutes from the city council meeting the night the issue was considered indicates that the council members had serious reservations about the administrative change, but voted for the change because "the seniors have demonstrated their aggressiveness." The final victory for the club came when the council agreed to call the new commission the Commission on Senior Citizens, a label that referred to them personally, rather than the Commission on Aging, language more in line with the problem orientation of the professionals.

Only a minority, but a very vocal minority, of the participants at the Center was involved in attempting to directly confront the postadult status attributed to them. Throughout the period of data collection, they continued to criticize the Center and the staff. Confrontations, some more disruptive than others, were a part of each day. A number of the most vocal critics withdrew altogether, planning special activities that only the chosen were invited to attend. A more common strategy used by the participants to protect self-identity, however, was to use role distance in the setting.

Role Distance

Most of the participants who used the Center, although they did not engage in confrontation, did not consider themselves to be postadults. The participants, however, shared with the staff the social definition of those who used the Senior Center *qua* senior center. To illustrate, a woman making inquiries about activities at the Center explained, "I guess I'm down to that point myself." Another old woman, incidentally, the only woman at the Center who aggressively adopted a "helpless old woman" role, stated, "If we weren't so old and sick, we wouldn't be down here." However, most other participants did not feel that they, personally, fit the stereotype of a senior citizens center participant; that is, that they were so old and sick that they were no longer able to plan for themselves.

In dealing with the conflict with the club, the supervisor, with all the bureaucratic strength he could muster, attempted to maintain his vision that the Center was "for all old people, not just for club members." He planned, or instructed the activities coordinator to plan, a number of recreational activities, craft demonstrations, and discussion groups. Club-sponsored activities were well attended while Center-sponsored activities were often cancelled. An explanation for the popularity of club activities is that club members were able to use role distance (Goffman, 1961).

> Role distance is a label for the myriad of concrete behaviors by means of which the person expresses [her or] himself to be something more than and something different from what the momentary, situated self defines him [or her] as being. . . . Such pointed expressions of incomplete acceptance of the moment serve subtly to inject other realities in a contained manner [Lofland, 1976: 119].

Old people who came to the Center came to do for others or to do with others, not to be done unto. For example, one woman brought flowers to share on days when special club activities were planned. Another was the self-appointed coffee maker. Another made cleaning the small kitchen her job. Club potlucks to which each participant brought a dish were popular. Group efforts which produced quilts or other items that could be used to raise money for the club were successful. Conflict arose among the participants when there were not enough "doer" roles to go around. For example, one old woman stormily withdrew from the Center when it became clear that she would not be allowed to be in charge of the kitchen.

By participating at the Center, they were filling the role of "senior citizens," but they made clear to others that they were much more than their situated selves would indicate. They made humorous and derogatory remarks about others who were "obviously" typical senior citizens. They pointed out their other daily and weekly pursuits that indicated that they were very busy people, unlike "real" old people, and that participating in this activity at the Center was just that—interest in one activity. They usually came in with friends and stayed with friends thereby presenting themselves as friends rather than as senior citizens. Women who came to the Center to play bridge, for example, were usually part of a foursome who met to play together. Old persons waiting at the Center for the bus for a ride home, made clear that they were merely waiting, not participating. Adult education classes, one of the few popular activities arranged by the staff at the Center, allowed participants to be students rather than senior citizens. With the exception of a few regulars, all who came saw themselves as primarily other persons than their situated selves would indicate and verbally and physically worked to maintain that image.[5]

Research on senior center participants consistently points to the small percentage, usually about five percent, of the eligible persons who actually avail themselves of the services (Carp, 1976; Hanssen et al., 1978; Trela and Simmons, 1971; Harris, 1975; Bild and Havighurst, 1976). In addition, "elderly people least in need of senior center services are those who use them most" (Carp, 1976: 224). Part of the explanation is that rewards available at a senior center are only great enough for those old persons who can successfully exercise role distance in the setting. When they have "gotten to that point," as the informant above stated, where they no longer feel capable of planning for themselves and have lost belief in and support for their other, higher status identities, then participating in activities at a senior center is too burdensome. One way for the old to protect their self-images of middle-aged is to avoid participating in groups, to avoid interaction with others who will define their oldness as pivotal. It should come as no surprise then that "Senior Centers appear to attract the less depressed, more active, and more physically intact older person" (Hanssen et al., 1978: 197). In the language of the theory presented here, senior centers attract primarily persons who can successfully use role distance, thereby escaping the pejorative implications of participating in senior center activities.

The Power of Professionals

In the resolution of the conflict between the social identity of the old promoted by gerontologized professionals and the self-identity held by the old themselves, the professionals have the upper hand. The use of role distance by the old is an individual adaptation to a personally threatening situation and is not a challenge to the imputations of the professionals. The victories won by the old through confrontation were only Pyrrhic. These tactics were easily defined by those with decision-making power as confirmation of the social image of the aged they already held. The old people's behavior was seen as irrational—a case of overreacting and not being able to see that those with power were working in their best interest. The old who engaged in confrontation were seen as cranks and troublemakers with too much time on their hands who blew minor issues out of proportion, further evidence of their nonadult status. Concessions were made to them not because those in power saw that the old were, afterall, responsible adults who were making rational arguments, but because it was the easiest way to cool them out (Goffman, 1952; Clark, 1960).

It is not simply in this specific case that the gerontologized professionals will win. They will win on a societal level as well. By establishing a network of services for the old under the Older Americans Act, a group of gerontological professionals and quasi-professionals has been created and the social identity of the old that they promote has been legitimated.

> The lay public by and large adopts the professional perspective for its major concern is to believe that others can be trusted to handle these problems which are potentially threatening to them but not a part of their everyday lives. This public reaction is the politically crucial one, for it confers power upon professionals and spreads their norms to others (Edelman, 1977: 67-68).

Further, this image of the aged promoted by the professionals may come to be a part of the self-identities of the old. The passage of time has a way of making new ideas, new constructions of reality, concrete and taken-for-granted.

> Thus, in the long run, the professionals who research, legislate, plan or implement interventions for the elderly, influence how different individuals *experience* the aging process. Social researchers, planners, and practitioners involved in intervention programs are not neutrals. Rather, they are actively engaged in modifying and structuring social reality for the aged [Estes and Freeman, 1976: 539].

Applied gerontologists and social service delivery workers may argue that the aged are so comparatively disadvantaged that the goal of making life easier for them justifies all efforts toward this end, regardless of a few detrimental unintended consequences. This is similar to the argument that applying the medical model to behaviorally aberrant behavior benefited the "mentally ill." It will be sad indeed if fifty years hence we must call on a new Szasz (1961) to point out the consequences of laying on the elderly a supposedly benign social identity.

Summary and Forecast

In the preceding chapters, the social worlds of old widows have been presented using as focal points those situations in their daily lives that pose problems to maintenance of an acceptable self-identity. The perspective has been primarily that of social actors. However, analysis began with a review of the historic and demographic changes that have affected the current social position of the aged. While both the number and proportion of the aged in the population have increased during this century, industrialization and the social legislation of the 1930s have combined to make the aged economically dependent members of society. Forced dependency is legitimated by the assumption that biological aging is an inevitable process of physical and mental deterioration. By drawing on past research, three components of the stereotype of an old person were assessed, that is, that s/he is poor, isolated, and unhealthy. The assumption of ill health, which has been used to legitimate institutionalization of the first two components, was presented as the most damaging to the self and social identities of the aged.

Following the presentation of the structural constraints with which the aged must deal in their everyday worlds, analysis shifted to a micro-level. In turning to a social-psychological perspective, the most salient feature of being old was presented as "uncertainty." The lack of a rite of passage that places people in the age category "old" and the lack of norms and expectations that prescribe "old" behavior in American society combine to place old persons in ambiguous social situations. Oldness is a stigma, but because of these absences it is a "weak" stigma. These factors combine to make self-identity and self-presentation problematic. A further complication is that the old share with other members of society the stereotypical view of old people. The social ambiguity involved in deciding to whom the label applies allows old women to take the option of defining themselves as "not old."

Even though an old woman may not think of herself as old, she must interact with others who think of her as old. In addition, having internalized the stereotypes that author negative expectations of "old" behavior, she may find evidence in her own behavior that she is, after all, an old woman. The strategies used to protect self-image in encounters with others and in encounters with self were presented.

The distinction between newcomers, those who come to a setting already old, and residents, those who age in a setting, was made, and the consequences to self-identity for each were shown. The subjective nature of belonging in a place was most obvious to the informants who were newcomers and had lost this feeling. The strategies available to the old women for protecting self-identity were shown to be limited because the Grim Reaper and changing physical and social environments are difficult to control.

In the discussion of the old widow's position in the family, analysis went beyond past research which has shown the existence of an extended family structure in American society to discover the subtler aspects of the relationships between old, widowed mothers and their offspring. The old mother's offspring are of primary importance to her for moral support. However, the old mother's relationship with her offspring may be viewed as the most important relationship in her life at the same time that her place in her children's lives has become ritualized. Placing this within an exchange framework, the relationship was described as unbalanced with respect to power because alternative ways to obtain the moral support and services available in the relationship with offspring are seen by the old mother as unacceptable, unavailable, or both. She may use strategies for balancing power, but for the most part her power resources were shown to be so limited that compliance with offspring's expectations was her best strategy.

The final problematic situation discussed was close temporal proximity to dying and being dead. The uncertainty of the how and when of death and dying was shown to be a recurrent theme for old women, and the strategies old women use to maintain an acceptable self-image at a future time when they will not have control over their self-presentations were outlined.

In this final chapter the level of analysis moved from the old widows' definitions of their worlds to focus on interaction between the participants and the staff of a senior citizens center. The staff, as imputational specialists, were shown to actively promote a definition of the participants as post-adults while the participants, through confrontation and role distance, attempted to maintain their definitions of themselves as adult members of society. It was suggested that the strategies used by the participants, while successful in the immediate situation, would be unsuccessful in the long run because of the power imputational specialists have been given to define the situation of being old in American society.

Throughout the book reference has been made to the similarities between the positions in which old widows find themselves and the problematic situations other social actors face for two related reasons. First is that the old are social actors and as such are subject to social forces in the same way that other social actors are. Too often research on the old explicitly or implicitly postulates that the old, because of their age and implied physical and mental decline, are not capable of reacting but are merely acted upon by societal forces. Borrowing from Warner et al. (1973: 74), "The key error of the earlier conception was to suppose that action undertaken under the force of circumstances was an accurate reflection of the being of the actor." The second reason for pointing out similarities is that this research is not merely a case study of old widows, but an in-depth sociological analysis of how actors manage to hold on to precarious self-images. Analysis of old widows' strategies will add to the growing body of literature on how actors in general maintain identity in problematic situations.

There is a very real possibility that imputed mental and physical incompetence may become the future norm for old age and that the old may actually begin to fit the stereotype just as adolescents now behave like "adolescents" (Mead, 1953). One piece of evidence that supports this assertion is the response of one informant who was a member of a senior citizens advisory board. She was assigned the task of looking into bills affecting older persons currently being considered in the state legislature. At the next meeting she commented that most of the bills were not just for the old, but also for the blind and disabled. She was amazed and incredulous that anyone would consider appropriate the lumping of the three groups together. As time passes this idea that was once new may, if it has not already, become part of a taken-for-granted world view. Forty years after the Social Security Act became law very few people find lumping the aged, blind, and disabled together surprising: the assumption is that to be old *is* to be handicapped. Younger persons are unaware that the "welfare state" has a history and may have "post-1930s" expectations about what being old should be. The social definition of old age promoted by the Older Americans Act and implemented by "gerontologized" imputational specialists may come to be more acceptable to succeeding cohorts of the old. There are other possibilities, however, and they are much more likely given the tenacity with which the old hold to their self-identities of "not old."

In comparing the strategies the informants use to maintain acceptable self-identities, the overriding similarity among them is that they all lead to increased social isolation. The powerlessness stemming from roles with no content and lack of economic resources, and the possession of a discrediting attribute, combine to make self-presentation problematic.

Internalization of the stereotypes about old age and beliefs about importance of family limit acceptable options for participation in social life. Indeed, they blind the old widows to possible options. There are two forces operating within society today which may serve to increase the visibility of options. Both are outgrowths of the Civil Rights Movement of the 1960s. Most obvious is the formation of the Gray Panthers, a group led by Maggie Kuhn, whose members view themselves as political activists fighting to abolish, the stigma of old age and to improve the economic and social position of the aged. How many of her followers understand the implications of ageism is not known; there is some indication that the most active participants are not the aged themselves, but social service professionals. However, if Piven and Cloward (1971) are right, old people who "take to the streets" to demonstrate their disfavor while pointing out their power as voters may successfully change the system to their advantage.

The second force which may prove important in pointing out options is the Women's Movement. There has been an increase in information about the oppression of women in society, and, although most of the appeal is probably to professional and young women, some of the ideas may be widely disseminated. A journal which has been in existence for several years, *Prime Time,* whose subscribers are women in the "prime of life," has been publishing articles about the effects of both ageism and sexism, including articles on "motherism" (Brabec, 1975). The Women's Movement focuses primarily on the effects of sexism, but discrimination based on age is intimately tied to discrimination based on gender (Sontag, 1972). Old women may benefit as effects become clearer and more widely publicized.

As visibility of options increases, the actual number of options may also increase, the cause once again being the social interpretation of demographic change.

The population over 65 is expected to continue to show substantial percentage increases for the next few decades (16 to 18%), although smaller increases than before 1970. . . . Early in the next century (2010 to 2020) the numbers of the aged will leap forward (30%) as these cohorts ["baby boom," 1945-1957] attain age 65. . . . The projected numbers of older persons cited here should be close to the mark because they are unaffected by future fertility [Siegel, 1972: 18-19].

In the next fifty years, then, an increase in the number and, very likely, the proportion of persons aged 65 and over is expected. Currently there is much attention focused on the consequences of an "aging" society in the popular media, as well as in Congress, and in discussions by social scientists (Neugarten and Havighurst, 1976) and, in particular, by economists who are concerned with issues such as the use of the increasing amount of capital in pension funds (Drucker, 1976). Congress's concern, and the general public's, is with the viability of the Social Security System. The spectre of an increasing percentage of the population retired and "living off" young workers is haunting members of American society. Pointing out that the "dependency ration," more realistically calculated as the number of persons under 19 and over 64 over the number of persons between these ages, will not be affected, does little to alleviate anxiety. Sharing income with spouses and children is one thing; helping to support retired persons, relatives, or nonrelatives, is quite another.

What effect will this have on the status of the aged? Here analysis becomes somewhat speculative as is always the case when predicting future events. However, a careful examination of the way in which Congress is dealing with the Social Security "crisis" indicates that there is currently a shift from an emphasis on what the aged *cannot* do to what the aged *can* do.[6] The goal is to find a way to reduce the amount of "dependency" of the old. One obvious way to reduce legally the number of old persons is to eliminate the universalistic criterion of age in order to link retirement to the more specific criterion of ability. Thus, current discussions of revisions of the Social Security Act include encouraging the aged to participate in the labor force, and recent legislation made mandatory retirement legal only after age 70 for most occupational groups. There is a real possibility that specific retirement age will be eliminated altogether.

As economists are quick to point out (Schulz, 1976a), this solution will probably change the ratio of workers to nonworkers so little that it can hardly be touted as a solution. Most workers will probably choose to retire "on schedule," that is, between the ages of 60 and 65. However, economic forces and their social interpretation are rarely synonymous. If they were, sociologists would have little to do. Elimination of chronological age as the legal criterion of the beginning of old age, while it may have minimal economic effects, may have far-reaching effects on the social definitions of the aged. If the aged are thought capable of and are expected to contribute to the economy, their credibility may increase and their confidence that the self they are presenting will receive support from others may increase concomitantly.

The issue raised here is not whether workers in American society will be able to support an increasing number of persons in the population that will be over sixty-five years of age. Clearly they can. As Rosow (1962) points out, the social position of the aged is a moral dilemma, not an economic one. Rather, the issue is whether or not American workers will see such support as legitimate. My prediction is that thirty percent will be seen as too much of a burden and at least some portion of the old will be welcomed back or welcomed into the labor force. The criterion may still be chronological age, but the age at which someone is legally old will be 70 or 75. The old will have the opportunity to participate in the ongoing social and economic order, in which case poverty and isolation may no longer be the accepted norm for as many of the old as is currently the case. However, the social identity of the old who cannot participate for whatever reason may continue to be spoiled.

NOTES

1. The following analysis is based in part on a paper entitled "Negotiation by Default: The Social Definition of Old Widows" which was prepared for presentation at the Society for the Study of Social Problems meetings, Chicago, 1977.

2. A major criticism of research on the elderly is that it is noncomparative. Very few studies are made of young adults or middle-aged adults to determine their "unmet needs." A recent poll conducted by Lou Harris and Associates (1975) is a notable exception. It may very well be that the "unmet needs" that accompany old age are present throughout life or are preferable to the ones faced earlier in life.

3. Lemert (1967: 202) states that spurious interaction is "distinguished by patronizing, evasion, 'humoring,' guiding conversations onto selected topics, underreaction, and silence. The net effects of spurious interaction are to:

1. Stop the flow of information to ego;
2. Create a discrepancy between expressed ideas and affect among those with whom he interacts;
3. Make the institution or the group's image an ambiguous one for ego, much as he is for others.

Needless to say this kind of spurious interaction is one of the most difficult for an adult in our society to cope with, because it complicates or makes decisions impossible for him and also because it is morally invidious."

4. "Needs assessment" surveys which are required by the Administration on Aging are usually nightmares for the social scientists involved. The stated purpose is to *assess* needs; the implicit purpose is to *find* needs and to involve "the elderly"—goals that are not in keeping with social scientists' definitions of science.

5. The role distance strategies for protecting self described here have been observed in other settings which are inherently discrediting to participants. Berk (1977) describes very similar strategies used by patrons at singles dances. There are, however, two important differences between senior centers and singles dances. Organizers of singles dances recognize that attendance is stigmatizing and work to redefine the situation positively, while organizers of senior centers, because of their view that the old are postadults, do not acknowledge that attendance is stigmatizing and often actively contribute to the negative image of the center. Second, the support each participant receives from other participants for assertions of "who s/he really is" varies. At senior centers in small communities or urban neighborhoods, participants are known to one another, often very well-known, and are more likely to support each other's assertions of "normality," while at singles dances support is much more difficult to negotiate.

6. I would like to thank Jackie L. Howsden for suggesting this conceptualization to me.

APPENDIX I-"HIRED HANDS" INTERVIEW GUIDE

No. _____

SMA Housing? _____ Date _____

Race or ethnicity _____ Time Started _____

Education _____ Time Ended _____

Social class _____ Interviewer _____

Age _____

Describe interview situation covering the following points:
1. the physical layout
2. respondent - was she
   a. difficult or easy to talk to?
   b. lucid or hazy in her descriptions?
   c. hiding things, straightforward, or telling all?

Record in writing conversation that isn't on the tape, giving special attention to references to old age.

No. _____
Date _____

ACTIVITIES

What does she do with her time?

FAMILY

Where relatives live
When she sees them
If she enjoys them
Does she feel dependent on them?
Sees her relationship as good or bad?

FRIENDS

Activities with friends
Age of Friends
Friends' deaths

STRANGERS - STEREOTYPED

Do strangers/casual acquaintances treat her condescending-
ly?

RETIREMENT

Was retirement (hers or her husband's) a problem?
Is being a widow difficult?
Thoughts on dying

COMPARED TO OTHERS HER AGE

How satisfactory does she think her life *is* compared to others her age?

GRANDMOTHER

Does she remember her grandmother? If yes, how does she think her life compares with her grandmother's?

YOUNGER PEOPLE

Any thoughts she may have about young people
Any relationships she has with young people

APPENDIX II-INTERVIEW GUIDE

Who are the people you see most often?   AGES

RELATIVES

FRIENDS

What does _____ usually call you? (name, mother, grand-mother, etc.)

What do you do with _____?

When you are with _____ what do you usually talk about?

Do you avoid talking about some things with _____?

Do you think that _____ avoids talking about some things with you?

Are there some things that _____ says or does that make you feel uncomfortable?

Have you noticed any difference in the way _____ treats you since you've gotten older?

Do you ever take advantage of your age when you are with _____?

Do you ever do things that you know _____ will disapprove of just to make a point?

Are there times when you feel very conscious of your age when you are with _____.

Are you ever surprised by what _____ expects of you?

Are there things you avoid doing with _____?

Do you think that _____ tries to do too much for you or makes too many decisions for you? Or not enough? Probe for equalitarian nature of relationship.

Do you sometimes feel that _____ treats you as if you were a child?

Do you ever think that _____ talks to you just to be polite?

Do you think of yourself as old when you are with _____?

Do you think _____ thinks of you as old?

Does walking alone or going places alone make you uneasy or nervous?

Has anyone ever made fun of you or harrassed you because of your age?

Are there recurrent questions that people you don't know well or meet for the first time ask you?

Do you have any trouble hearing?   seeing?
   When are you most conscious of this?
   With whom?
   Do you avoid going places because you cannot hear well?

Do you think of yourself as old, middle-aged, young or what?

Is there a particular old person that you admire very much?
DESCRIBE
   famous, friend, relative

Do you avoid going places where there are a lot of young people?

Do you think very much about dying?

Are there some things you would like to do but don't because you think it's inappropriate for a person your age to do them?

What do you like about being your age?

What do you dislike about being your age?

Do you remember having any ideas about what it would be like to be over seventy when you were younger?

Do you avoid going out at night?

Do you depend on others for transportation?

REFERENCES

Adams, Bert N., 1968, "The Middle-Class Adult and His Widowed or Still-Married Mother." Social Problems 16(1):50-59.

Adams, David L., 1971, "Correlates of Satisfaction Among the Elderly." The Gerontologist 11(4,2):64-68.

Administration on Aging, 1976, Older Americans Act of 1965 as Amended and Related Acts. Washington, D.C.: Government Printing Office.

Allan, Virginia R., 1975, "Economic and Legal Status of the Older Woman." In No Longer Young: The Older Woman in America, Proceedings of the 26th Annual Conference on Aging. Ann Arbor: Institute of Gerontology, University of Michigan, Wayne State University, pp. 23-30.

Aries, Philippe, 1962, Centuries of Childhood: A Social History of Family Life. New York: Vintage.

Arth, Malcolm, 1962, "American Culture and the Phenomenon of Friendship in Old Age." In Clark Tibbitts and Wilma Donahue (eds.) Social and Psychological Aspects of Aging. New York: Columbia University Press, pp. 529-534.

Atchley, Robert C., 1972, The Social Forces in Later Life. Belmont, Ca.: Wadsworth.

———, 1976, The Sociology of Retirement. New York: Halstead.

Banton, Michael, 1965, Roles: An Introduction to the Study of Social Relations. New York: Basic Books.

Barker, Michael B., 1966, California Retirement Communities: Special Report No. 2. Center for Real Estate and Urban Economics, Institute of Urban and Regional Development. Berkeley: University of California.

Bart, Pauline, 1975, "The Emotional and Social Status of the Older Woman." In Natalie P. Trager (ed.) No Longer Young: The Older Woman in America. Ann Arbor, Michigan: Institute of Gerontology, pp. 3-21.

Beard, Belle B., 1949, "Are the Aged Ex-Family?" Social Forces 27:274-279.

Becker, Ernest, 1962, The Birth and Death of Meaning. New York: Free Press.

Beeson, Diane, 1975, "Women in Studies of Aging: A Critique and Suggestion." Social Problems 23(1):52-59.

Benson, Joseph, 1971, "Classical Music and the Status Game." In Irving Louis Horowitz and Mary Symons Strong (eds.) Sociological Realities: A Guide to the Study of Society. New York: Harper & Row, pp. 240-245.

Berger, Peter L., 1963, Invitation to Sociology. Garden City, N.Y.: Doubleday.
——— and Thomas Luckmann, 1967, The Social Construction of Reality. Garden City, N.Y.: Doubleday.
Berk, Bernard, 1977, "Face-Saving at the Singles Dance." Social Problems 24(5):530-544.
Barnard, Jessie, 1974, "Sex Differences: An Overview." New York: MSS Modular Publications, Module 26.
Bild, Bernice and Robert J. Havighurst, 1976, "Senior Citizens in Great American Cities: The Case of Chicago." The Gerontologist 16(1,2).
Binstock, Robert H., 1972, "Interest-Group Liberalism and the Politics of Aging." The Gerontologist 12:265-280.
Birren, James E., Robert N. Butler, Samuel W. Greenhouse, L. Sokoloff, and Marian Yarrow, 1963, Human Aging: A Biological and Behavioral Study. National Institute of Mental Health, PHS Publication No. 986. Washington, D.C.: Government Printing Office.
Bixby, Lenore E., Wayne W. Ginegar, Susan Grad, Walter W. Kolodrubetz, Patience Laureat, and Janet Murray, 1975, Demographic and Economic Characteristics of the Aged: 1968 Social Security Survey. Social Security Administration, Office of Research and Statistics Research, Report No. 45. Washington, D.C.: Government Printing Office.
Blau, Peter M., 1964, Exchange and Power in Social Life. New York: John Wiley.
Blau, Zena Smith, 1956, "Changes in Age and Status Identification." American Sociological Review 21:198-203.
———, 1961, "Structural Constraints on Friendships in Old Age." American Sociological Review 26:429-439.
Blenkner, Margaret, 1965, "Social Work and Family Relationships in Later Life with Some Thoughts on Filial Maturity." In Ethel Shanas and Gordon Streib (eds.) Social Structure and the Family: Generational Relations. Englewood Cliffs, N.J.: Prentice Hall, pp. 46-59.
Booth, Alan and Henry Camp, 1974, "Housing Relocation and Family Social Integration Patterns." Journal of the American Institute of Planners 40(2):124-128.
Brabec, Bette Dewing, 1975, "Motherism: A Cause for Despair and Madness." Prime Time 3(2):7ff.
———, 1976, "Generations Apart." Prime Time 4(3):8-9ff.
Brody, Elaine M., 1971, "Aging." In Encyclopedia of Social Work 16(1). New York: National Association of Social Workers, pp. 51-74.
Brotman, Herman B., 1971, Facts and Figures on Older Americans, No. 5, An Overview. Washington, D.C.: Administration on Aging, Office of Human Development, U.S. Department of Health, Education and Welfare.
Brown, J. Douglas, 1950, "The Role of Industry in Relation to the Older Worker." In Milton Derber (ed.) The Aged and Society. Champaign, Ill.: Industrial Relations Research Association, pp. 65-74.
Brubaker, Timothy H. and Edward A. Powers, 1976, "The Stereotype of 'Old': A Review and Alternative Approach." Journal of Gerontology 31(4):441-447.
Burgess, Ernest W., 1960, Aging in Western Societies: A Comparative Survey. Chicago: University of Chicago Press.

References

Butler, Robert N., 1968, "The Facade of Chronological Age." In Bernice L. Neugarten (ed.) Middle Age and Aging. Chicago; University of Chicago Press, pp. 235-246.

Carp, Frances M., 1972, "Retired People as Automobile Passengers." The Gerontologist 12(1):66-72.

———, 1976, "A Senior Center in Public Housing for the Elderly." The Gerontologist 16(3):243-249.

Clark, Burton R., 1960, "The 'Cooling-Out' Function of Higher Education." American Journal of Sociology 66:569-576.

Clark, Margaret and Barbara G. Anderson, 1967, Culture and Aging: An Anthropological Study of Older Americans. Springfield, Ill.: Charles C Thomas.

Confrey, Eugene and Marcus S. Goldstein, 1969, "The Health Status of Aging People." In Clark Tibbitts (ed.) Handbook of Social Gerontology. Chicago: University of Chicago Press, pp. 165-207.

Cooley, Charles H., 1967, "Looking-Glass Self." In Jerome G. Manis and Bernard N. Miltzer (eds.) Symbolic Interaction: A Reader in Social Psychology. Boston, Mass.: Allyn & Bacon, pp. 217-219.

Cooley, Leland Frederick and Lee Morrison Cooley, 1965, The Retirement Trap. Garden City, N.Y.: Doubleday.

Coombs, Robert H. and Lawrence J. Goldman, 1973, "Maintenance and Discontinuity of Coping Mechanisms in an Intensive Care Unit." Social Problems 20:342-355.

Corning, Peter A., 1969, The Evolution of Medicare: From Idea to Law. Washington, D.C.: Government Printing Office.

Coser, Rose, 1974, The Family: Its Structures and Functions. New York: St. Martin's.

Cottrell, Fred, 1969, "The Technological and Societal Basis of Aging." In Clark Tibbitts (ed.) Handbook of Social Gerontology. Chicago: University of Chicago Press.

Cowgill, Donald O., 1972, "Aging in American Society." In Donald O. Cowgill and Lowell D. Holmes (eds.) Aging and Modernization. New York: Appleton Century Crofts, pp. 92-119.

———, 1974, "Aging and Modernization: A Revision of the Theory." In Jaber Gubrium (ed.) Late Life: Communities and Environmental Policy. Springfield, Ill.: Charles C Thomas, pp. 123-146.

——— and Lowell D. Holmes, 1972, Aging and Modernization. New York: Appleton-Century-Crofts.

Cumming, Elaine and William E. Henry, 1961, Growing Old. New York: Basic Books.

Davis, Fred, 1961, "Deviance Disavowal: The Management of Strained Interaction by the Visibly Handicapped." Social Problems 9:120-132.

de Beauvoir, Simone, 1972, The Coming of Age. New York: Basic Books.

Deutscher, Irwin, 1962, "Socialization for Postparental Life." In Arnold M. Rose (ed.) Human Behavior and Social Processes. Boston: Houghton Mifflin, pp. 506-525.

———, 1973, What We Say/What We Do: Sentiments and Acts. Glenview, Ill.: Scott, Forseman.

Donahue, Wilma, Harold L. Orbach, and Otto Pollak, 1960, "Retirement: The Emerging Social Pattern." In Clark Tibbitts (ed.) Handbook of Social Gerontology. Chicago: University of Chicago Press, pp. 330-406.

Douglas, Jack, 1974, Understanding Everyday Life. London: Routledge & Kegan Paul.

Dowd, James P., 1975, "Aging as Exchange: A Preface to Theory." Journal of Gerontology 30(5):584-594.

Doyle, Joseph T., 1972, "Other Physiologic Changes with Age—Discussant's Perspective." In Adrian M. Ostfeld and Donald C. Gibbons (eds.) Epidimeology of Aging. Washington, D.C.: Government Printing Office, pp. 157-160.

Drake, Joseph T., 1957, "Some Factors Influencing Students' Attitudes Toward Older People." Social Forces 35(3):266-270.

Drucker, Peter, 1976, The Unseen Revolution: How Pension Fund Socialism Came to America." New York: Harper & Row.

Duvall, Evelyn M., 1954, In-Laws—Pro and Con: An Original Study of Interpersonal Relations. New York: Association Press.

Edelman, Murray, 1977, "The Political Language of the Helping Professions." In Political Language: Words that Succeed and Policies that Fail. New York: Academic Press, pp. 57-75.

Emerson, Robert M., 1962, "Power-Dependence Relations." American Sociological Review 27:31-41.

Erikson, Kai T., 1976, "Trauma at Buffalo Creek." Society 13(6):58-65.

Estes, Carroll, 1973, "Community Planning for the Elderly from an Organizational, Political, and Interactionist Perspective." Ph.D. dissertation, Department of Sociology, University of California, San Diego.

——— and Howard E. Freeman, 1976, "Strategies of Design and Research for Intervention." In Robert H. Binstock and Ethel Shanas (eds.) Handbook of Aging and the Social Sciences. New York: Van Nostrand-Reinhold, pp. 536-560.

Fischer, David Hackett, 1977, Growing Old in America. New York: Oxford University Press.

——— and Lawrence Stone, 1977, "Growing Old: An Exchange." New York Review of Books, September 15, pp. 47-49.

Fishman, Pamela, 1978, "Interaction: The Work Women Do." Social Problems 25(4):395-406.

Fran, Forrest, Spes of Cabbage Lane, 1974, "Can't Let Your Kids Run Your Life." Country Women, July, pp. 30-31.

Fried, Marc, 1963, "Grieving for a Lost Home." In Leonard J. Duhl (ed.) The Urban Condition: People and Policy in Metropolis. New York: Basic Books, pp. 151-171.

Friedmann, Eugene A., 1960, "The Impact of Aging on the Social Structure." In Clark Tibbitts (ed.) Handbook of Social Gerontology. Chicago: University of Chicago Press, pp. 120-144.

Glaser, Barney G. and Anselm L. Strauss, 1967, The Discovery of Grounded Theory: Strategies for Qualitative Research. Chicago: Aldine.

Goffman, Erving, 1952, "Cooling the Mark Out: Some Aspects of Adaptation to Failure." Psychiatry 15:451-463.

References

———, 1959, Presentation of Self in Everyday Life. Garden City, N.Y.: Double-day-Anchor.

———, 1961, Encounters: Two Studies in the Sociology of Interaction. Indianapolis: Bobbs-Merrill.

———, 1963, Stigma: Notes on the Management of Spoiled Identity. Englewood Cliffs, N.J.: Prentice-Hall.

Gold, Byron D., 1974, "The Role of the Federal Government in the Provision of Social Services to Older Persons." The Annals of the American Academy 415:55-69.

Goode, William, 1963, World Revolution and Family Patterns. New York: Free Press.

Gubrium, Jaber, 1975, "On Being Single in Old Age." International Journal of Aging and Human Development 6(1): 29-41.

Hanssen, Anne M., Nicholas J. Meima, Linda M. Buckspan, Barbara E. Henderson, Thea L. Helbig, and Steven H. Zarit., 1978, "Correlates of Senior Center Participation." The Gerontologist 18(2): 193-199.

Hareven, Tamara K., 1977, "Family Time and Historical Time." Daedalus 106(2):57-70.

Harris, Lou and Associates, 1975, The Myth and Reality of Aging in America. Washington, D.C.: The National Council on the Aging, Inc.

Hochschild, Arlie Russell, 1969, "A Community of Grandmothers." Ph.D. dissertation, Department of Sociology, University of California, Berkeley.

———, 1973, The Unexpected Community. Englewood Cliffs, N.J.: Prentice-Hall.

Homans, George C., 1958, "Social Behavior as Exchange." American Journal of Sociology 63:596-606.

Isenberg, Barbara, 1972, "Out to Pasture: To be Old and Poor is to Be Alone, Afraid, Ill-Fed, and Unknown." Wall Street Journal, November 15, pp. 1ff.

Jackman, Norman R., Richard O'Toole, and Gilbert Geis, 1963, "The Self-Image of the Prostitute." Sociological Quarterly 4:150-160.

Johnson, Sheila K., 1971, Idle Haven: Community Building Among the Working Class Retired: Berkeley: University of California Press.

Karp, David A., Gregory P. Stone, and William C. Yoels, 1977, Being Urban: A Social Psychological View of City Life. Lexington, Mass.: D.C. Heath.

Kastenbaum, Robert and Nancy Durkee, 1964, "Elderly People View Old Age." In Robert Kastenbaum (ed.) New Thoughts on Old Age. New York: Springer Publishing, pp. 250-262.

Keller, Suzanne, 1971, "Does the Family Have a Future?" Journal of Comparative Family Studies, Spring.

Kessler, Suzanne J. and Wendy McKenna, 1978, Gender: An Ethnomethodological Approach. New York: John Wiley.

Kett, Joseph, 1977, Rites of Passage: Adolescence in America. New York: Basic Books.

Kitsuse, John I., 1962, "Societal Reaction to Deviant Behavior." Social Problems 9:247-256.

Komarovsky, Mirra, 1962, Blue Collar Marriage. New York: Random House.

Komisar, Lucy, 1974, Down and Out in the USA: A History of Social Welfare. New York: New Viewpoints.

Lakoff, Sanford A., 1976, "The Future of Social Intervention." In Robert H. Binstock and Ethel Shanas (eds.) Handbook of Aging and the Social Sciences. New York: Van Nostrand-Reinhold, pp. 643-663.

Lancaster, Hal, 1972, "Out to Pasture: The Old but Affluent Withdraw to Sun City to Fill Empty Days." Wall Street Journal, November 16, pp. 1ff.

Lee, Dorothy, 1950, "Lineal and Non-Lineal Codifications of Reality." Psychosomatic Medicine 12:89-97.

Lemert, Edwin M., 1967, "Paranoia and the Dynamics of Exclusion." In Human Deviance, Social Problems and Social Control. Englewood Cliffs, New Jersey: Prentice-Hall.

Lemon, Bruce W., Vern L. Bengston, and James A. Peterson, 1973, "An Exploration of the Activity Theory of Aging: Activity Types and Life Satisfaction Among In-Movers to a Retirement Community." Journal of Gerontology 27(4):511-523.

Lifton, Robert Jay, 1969, Death in Life: Survivors of Hiroshima. New York: Vintage.

Litwak, Eugene, 1961, "Occupational Mobility and Extended Family Cohesion." American Sociological Review 25:9-27.

Lofland, John, 1969, Deviance and Identity. Englewood Cliffs, N.J.: Prentice-Hall.

———, 1971, Analyzing Social Settings: A Guide to Qualitative Observation and Analysis. Belmont, Ca.: Wadsworth.

———, 1976, Doing Social Life. New York: John Wiley.

Lofland, Lyn H., 1973, A World of Strangers: Order and Action in Urban Public Space. New York: Basic Books.

Lopata, Helena Z., 1970, "The Social Involvement of American Widows." American Behavioral Scientist 14(1):41-57..

———, 1973, Widowhood in an American City. Cambridge, Mass.: Schenkman.

Lowenthal, Marjorie Fiske and Clayton Haven, 1968, "Interaction and Adaptation: Intimacy as a Critical Variable." In Bernice L. Neugarten (ed.) Middle Age and Aging. Chicago: University of Chicago Press, pp. 390-400.

Lyman, Stanford B. and Marvin B. Scott, 1970, "Accounts." In A Sociology of the Absurb. New York: Appleton-Century-Crofts, pp. 111-143.

McClendon, McKee J., 1976, "The Occupational Status Attainment Processes of Males and Females." American Sociological Review 4(1):52-64.

McTavish, Donald G., 1971, "Perceptions of Old People: A Review of Research Methodologies." The Gerontologist 11(4):74-78.

Marshall, Victor, 1975, "Socialization for Impending Death in a Retirement Village:" American Journal of Sociology 80:1124-1144.

Masaro, Edward, 1972, "Other Physiologic Changes with Age." In Adrian M. Ostfeld and Donald C. Gibbons (eds.) Epidimeology of Aging. Washington, D.C.: Government Printing Office, pp. 140-156.

Mead, George Herbert, 1970, Mind, Self, and Society. Chicago: University of Chicago Press.

Mead, Margaret, 1953, Mead, George Herbert, The Coming of Age in Samoa. New York: Modern Library.

References

Moore, Wilbert E., 1950, "The Aged in Industrial Society." In Milton Derber (ed.) The Aged and Society. Champaign, Ill.: Industrial Relations Association, pp. 24-39.

Musgrove, Frank, 1965, Youth and the Social Order. Bloomington, Ind.: Indiana University Press.

Neugarten, Bernice, 1966, "The Aged in American Society." In Howard S. Becker (ed.) Social Problems. New York: John Wiley.

——— and Robert J. Havighurst, 1976, Social Policy, Social Ethics, and the Aging Society. Washington, D.C.: Government Printing Office.

Nimkoff, M.F., 1962, "Changing Family Relationships of Older People in the United States During the Last Fifty Years." In Clark Tibbits and Wilma Donahue (eds.) Social and Psychological Aspects of Aging. New York: Columbia University Press, pp. 405-414.

Parsons, Talcott, 1942, "Age and Sex in the Social Structure of the United States." American Sociological Review 7:604-616.

———, 1963, "Death in American Society: A Brief Working Paper." American Behavioral Scientist 6:61-65.

Pauley, Gay, 1973, "Why Not Have a Grandparents' Day?" The Davis Enterprise. June 7, p. 5.

Phillips, Bernard, 1957, "A Role Theory Approach to Adjustment in Old Age." American Sociological Review 22(2):212-217.

Piven, Frances Fox and Richard A. Cloward, 1971, Regulating the Poor: The Functions of Public Welfare. New York: Vintage Books.

Polanyi, Michael, 1967, The Tacit Dimension. New York: Anchor Books.

Preston, C.E., 1968, "Subjectively Perceived Agedness and Retirement." Journal of Gerontology 23:201-204.

Putnam, Jackson K., 1970, Old Age Politics in California: From Richardson to Reagan. Palo Alto, California: Stanford University Press.

Ray, Marsh B., 1961, "The Cycle of Abstinence and Relapse Among Heroin Addicts." Social Problems 9:132-140.

Riley, Matilda White and Anne Foner, 1968, "The Family." In Matilda White Riley and Anne Foner (eds.) Aging and Society, Volume I: An Inventory of Findings. New York: Russell Sage Foundation, pp. 157-184.

Rose, Arnold, 1965, "The Subculture of Aging." In Arnold Rose and Warren Peterson (eds.) Older People and Their Social World. Philadelphia, Penn.: F. A. Davis, pp. 3-16.

Rosow, Irving, 1962, "Old Age: One Moral Dilemma of an Affluent Society." The Gerontologist 2:182-191.

———, 1967, Social Integration of the Aged. New York: Free Press.

———, 1974, Socialization to Old Age. Berkeley: University of California Press.

Ross, Jennie-Keith, 1977, Old People, New Lives: Community Creation in a Retirement Residence. Chicago: University of Chicago Press.

Roth, Julius, 1966, "Hired Hand Research." American Sociologist 1(4): 190-196.

Ryan, William, 1971, Blaming the Victim. New York: Pantheon Books.

Ryder, Norman B., 1974, "The Family in Developed Countries." Scientific American 231:122-128ff.

Sarbin, Theodore, 1968, "Notes on the Transformation of Social Identity." In Leigh M. Roberts, Norman S. Greenfield, and Milton H. Miller (eds.) Comprehensive Mental Health: The Challenge of Evaluation. Madison: University of Wisconsin Press, pp. 97-115.

Schorr, Alvin, 1960, Filial Responsibility in the Modern American Family. Washington, D.C.: Social Security Administration.

Schulz, James H., 1976a, The Economics of Aging. Belmont, CA: Wadsworth.

———, 1976b, "Income Distribution of the Aging." In Robert H. Binstock and Ethel Shanas (eds.) Handbook of Aging and the Social Sciences. New York: Van Nostrand-Reinhold.

Schutz, Alfred, 1964, "The Homecomer." In Collected Papers. The Hague: Nijoff, pp. 106-119.

Shanas, Ethel, 1962, The Health of Older People: A Social Survey. Cambridge, Mass.: Harvard University Press.

———, Peter Townsend, Dorothy Wedderburn, Paul Milhoj, and Jan Stenhouwer, 1968, Old People in Three Industrial Societies. New York: Atherton Press.

Shibutani, Tomatsu, 1961, Society and Personality: An Interactionist Approach to Social Psychology. Englewood Cliffs, N.J.: Prentice-Hall.

Siegel, Jacob S., 1972, "Some Demographic Aspects of Aging in the United States." In Adrian N. Ostfeld and Doanld C. Gibbons (eds.) Epidemeology of Aging. Washington, D.C.: Government Printing Office, pp. 17-82:

Simmel, Georg, 1950, "The Isolated Individual and the Dyad." In Kurt H. Wolff (ed.) The Sociology of Georg Simmel. New York: Free Press, pp. 118-144.

Simmons, Leo W., 1945, The Role of the Aged in Primitive Society. New Haven: Yale University Press.

Simon, Anne W., 1968, The New Years: A New Middle Age. New York: Alfred A. Knopf.

Smith, Bert Kruger, 1973, Aging in America. Boston, Mass.: Beacon Press.

Sontag, Susan, 1972, "The Double Standard of Aging." Saturday Review of Society 55(39):29-38.

Stone, Gregory P., 1975, "Appearance and the self." In Dennis Brissett and Charles Edgley (eds.) Life as Theater: A Dramaturgical Sourcebook. Chicago: Aldine, pp. 78-90.

Strauss, Anselm, 1959, Mirrors and Masks: The Search for Identity. Glencoe, Ill.: Free Press.

Sudnow, David, 1967, Passing On: The Social Organization of Dying. Englewood Cliffs, N.J.: Prentice-Hall.

Sussman, Marvin B., 1965, "Relationships of Adult Children with Their Parents in the United States." In Ethel Shanas and Gordon F. Streib (eds.) Social Structure and the Family. Englewood Cliffs, N.J.: Prentice-Hall, pp. 62-92.

——— and Lee Burchinal, 1962, "Kin Family Network: Unheralded Structure in Current Conceptualizations of Family Functioning." Marriage and Family Living 24(3):231-240.

Suttles, Gerald D., 1968, The Social Order of the Slum. Chicago: University of Chicago Press.

Szasz, Thomas, 1961, The Myth of Mental Illness. New York: Hoeber-Harper Books.

Taylor, Craig, 1971, "The 'Battered Child': Individual Victim of Family Brutality." In Clifton D. Bryant (ed.) Social Problems Today. Philadelphia: J.B. Lippincott.

tenBroek, Jacobus, 1964, "California's Dual System of Family Law: Its Origins, Development, and Present Status." Stanford Law Review 16:257-317.

Tissue, Thomas, 1972, Patterns of Aging on Welfare. Sacramento, Ca.: State of California, Human Relations Agency, Department of Social Welfare, July.

Townsend, Peter, 1957, The Family Life of Old People. London: Routledge & Kegan Paul.

———, 1963, "Measuring Incapacity for Self-Care." In Richard H. Williams, Clark Tibbitts and Wilma Donahue (eds.) Processes of Aging. New York: Atherton Press, pp. 269-288.

Travisano, Richard V., 1970, "Alternation and Conversion as Qualitatively Different Transformations." In Gregory P. Stone and Harvey Farberman (eds.) Social Psychology Through Symbolic Interaction. Waltham, Mass.: Ginn-Blaisdell, pp. 594-606.

Trela, J.E. and W. Simmons, 1971, "Health and Other Factors Affecting Membership and Attrition in a Senior Center." Journal of Gerontology 26:45-51.

Tuckman, Jacob and Irving Lorge, 1953, "Attitudes Toward Older People." Journal of Social Psychology 37:249-260.

van den Berghe, Pierre L., 1973, Age and Sex in Human Societies: A Biosocial Perspective. Belmont, Ca.: Wadsworth.

Warner, R. Stephen, David T. Wellman, and Lenore J. Weitzman, 1973, "The Hero, the Sambo, and the Operator." Urban Life and Culture 2(1): 53-84.

Weitzman, Lenore, 1974, "Marriage Contracts." California Law Review 62: 1170-1288.

Wilensky, Harold L., 1975, The Welfare State and Equality: Structural and Ideological Roots of Public Expenditures. Berkeley, Ca.: University of California Press.

Young, Michael and Hildred Geertz, 1961, "Old Age in London and San Francisco: Some Families Compared." British Journal of Sociology 12:124-141.

Zimmer, B.G., 1970, "Participation of Migrants in Urban Structures." In Clifford J. Jansen (ed.) Readings in the Sociology of Migration. New York: Pergamon Press, pp. 71-83.

AUTHOR INDEX